What Educators Are Saying About Vocab Rock

What Educators Are Saying About Vocab Rock

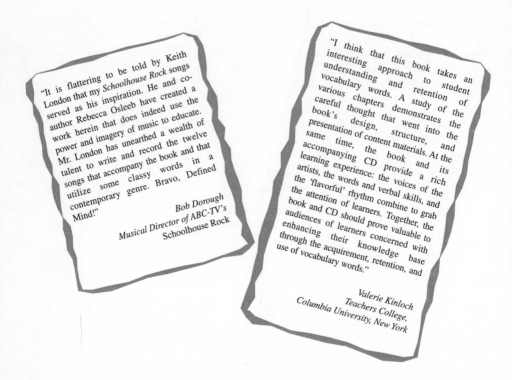

"It is flattering to be told by Keith London that my *Schoolhouse Rock* songs served as his inspiration. He and co-author Rebecca Osleeb have created a work herein that does indeed use the power and imagery of music to educate. Mr. London has unearthed a wealth of talent to write and record the twelve songs that accompany the book and that utilize some classy words in a contemporary genre. Bravo, Defined Mind!"

Bob Dorough
Musical Director of ABC-TV's
Schoolhouse Rock

"I think that this book takes an interesting approach to student understanding and retention of vocabulary words. A study of the various chapters demonstrates the careful thought that went into the book's design, structure, and presentation of content materials. At the same time, the book and its accompanying CD provide a rich learning experience: the voices of the artists, the words and verbal skills, and the 'flavorful' rhythm combine to grab the attention of learners. Together, the book and CD should prove valuable to audiences of learners concerned with enhancing their knowledge base through the acquirement, retention, and use of vocabulary words."

Valerie Kinloch
Teachers College,
Columbia University, New York

What Parents and Students Are Saying About Vocab Rock

Dear Defined Mind,

Hello from California, from one of your new fans of this absolutely fabulous idea. You have NO idea what impact this has had on my daughter of 13 and how in one 6-hour drive from L.A., we learned a song together. For that, I will forever be grateful. My daughter, for the first time in her life, used ephemeral in a sentence about a discussion she had, used it right and is damn proud about it. This is a breakthrough for us, for she is a Norwegian, and English has been a challenge. YOU have done something so great with this idea.

Thank you for your efforts in this field and for giving our young people a different, exciting approach to learning.

Stephanie

Dear Nina,

I want to thank you. Your song is awesome. It would be my greatest dream to sing with you. I am 13 and I'm in seventh grade and lots of kids at my school are having trouble with vocabulary, including me. I moved here from Norway about five years ago and it was always hard for me to spell and read. "Ephemeral Days" is the BEST SONG on the CD and even my mom likes it. I know almost all the words and meanings. People connect by songs and melody and your song really touched me and it's a wonderful song.

Warmly,

Katrina

"My son did very well on the SAT. Defined Mind gave him a lot of confidence on the test."

Paula Sullivan
Manasquan, New Jersey

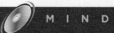

DEFINED MIND

VOCAB ROCK

Musical Prep for the SAT and ACT

Keith London
&
Rebecca Osleeb

THOMSON
PETERSON'S

Australia • Canada • Mexico • Singapore • Spain • United Kingdom • United States

Produced by Native LLC | Recorded @ Native, New York, NY, July–October 2004 |
29 West 17th St., NYC 10011 | www.nativemusic.net | KEITH LONDON, EXECUTIVE
PRODUCER | DAKOTA LONDON, BEST BOY | Produced with Robert Last

About Thomson Peterson's

Thomson Peterson's (www.petersons.com) is a leading provider of education information
and advice, with books and online resources focusing on education search, test prepara-
tion, and financial aid. Its Web site offers searchable databases and interactive tools for
contacting educational institutions, online practice tests and instruction, and planning
tools for securing financial aid. Thomson Peterson's serves 110 million education
consumers annually.

For more information, contact Thomson Peterson's, 2000 Lenox Drive, Lawrenceville,
NJ 08648; 800-338-3282; or find us on the World Wide Web at www.petersons.com/
about.

ISBN-13: 978-0-7689-2305-6
ISBN-10: 0-7689-2305-0

Printed in Canada

10 9 8 7 6 5 4 3 2 1   08 07 06

First Edition

Contents

Contents

Acknowledgments

I would like to thank the following professionals for their invaluable contributions to this work | Dr. Robert Strickland, Ph.D., Executive Director of the Miami-Dade, Florida, School District | Ms. Katherine Brennan, M.S., Education Liaison at the Rita & Stanley Kaplan Foundation | Mr. Lev Kaye, Executive Director, Kaplan Test Prep & Admissions | Ms. Laura Garner, M.S., Middle School & High School English Language Arts Coordinator for the Berkeley County School District

And many thanks to | Robin, my soul mate, for not divorcing me while I created An Alternate Reality | Dakota, my mini soul mate, for giving the studio a great Allman Brothers cover vibe | Grandpa, for making it possible—Granny would have loved it | Jemi, Dick & Fran, for Blood is Thickerer | The Artists who jumped at the chance to put their hearts & souls into this recording | Rebecca the Genius, for ditchin' pitchin' hoagies to work in the Penthouse or Style on the studio couch | The visionary Johnny Zed, who gave us the muscle to put it together | JT, for insight & keeping me on the right track | Nina, for her Passion & hooking up the studio | Dave, Craig & Mike, for buying in & getting it done | Michele, a Woman of Action | Steven Beer, Bill Glad, for Street Cred | Todd Retallack "i-dog," Rainer Jenss, Sue Maz, Markus Malarkus, Fantastic Dan, Mike Sweeney, Bob & Rodger, for their backing & Wise Counsel | Bennett, for telling Sue to 'Just Do It' | Jason, for rollin' the dice on hot dogs | Rudy, for his open door and great wisdom & tough love | & of course, The Reverend Gil, without you, Mia & The Band would still be hanging out on 17th Street, waiting for the elevator.

Read Me

We figured that there's a better way to study, and why not listen to beats while you're getting something done?

The people who put the *Vocab Rock* CD and guide together are independent recording artists who love music and teachers who love words. And you know you tend to need words when you're writing songs.

The *Vocab Rock* music includes vocabulary words that you'll need to learn for school, tests, life . . . but you won't notice them until you read the lyrics. After you listen to the CD, the exercises back up the tracks. A hint for you—GO TO THE ANSWER KEY IF YOU DON'T KNOW SOMETHING. There's no point to leaving a blank space, so you may as well find out what the answer is. If you look up a word, it's a good bet that you'll know it the next time you see it.

So, grab your headphones, get something to write with, and let's rock.

—Keith London

Listening Exercise

Listen to "Hot" all the way through at least once. Then listen to the song again, and graffiti up the wall with any new or unfamiliar words that you hear. Don't worry if you don't fill up the whole wall . . . we're not going to peruse your work . . .

HOT | Keith Middleton & Rodney Willie | Lyrics by Rodney Willie | Music Written & Performed by Keith Middleton | Vocals: Avon Marshall & Rodney Willie | Produced by Keith Middleton | Technical Producer: Craig Chang

LYRICS

| Got an e-mail that was sent to me | 'bout a party happening this week | It said we're required to be **SEDENTARY** | While we're in class sitting quietly | But not for long | We'll get you on your feet | We know you're tired of **UNIFORMITY** | Same old **MONOTONY** can make you weak | We can **RECTIFY** it | We've got the **REMEDY** | Raves of the party would **PROPAGATE** | Word was spreading quickly no one could wait | The girl I wanted to take seemed to **VACILLATE** | She kept **WAVERING** on who she wanted to date | Her **FLUCTUATION**, got so **FRUSTRATING**, I wasn't waiting | Said I'd go alone, then I got the message | From my best friend, "Yo! This party is hot!" | I hung up the phone | Hot | Temperature's changing | Hot | **IGNITED** and flaming | Hot | There's no mistaking | **CONFLAGRATION** fires **RAZING** | It's so **EXHILARATING**, exciting, **INVIGORATING** | Inviting and **STIMULATING** | I don't ever want to go | It was no **ILLUSION** | It was real and I was there | What a beautiful **UNION** | **FUSION** of the crowd and music so amusing | In the **PROXIMITY** of a girl sitting in **SECLUSION** | Her I'm **PERUSING**, **PURSUING**, I'm using a **PROFUSION** | Of **UNGAINLY** moves that made her laugh | Said I be doing much better with a partner | So I took her hand and we started to dance... | Hot | Temperature's changing | Hot | **IGNITED** and flaming | Hot | There's no mistaking | **CONFLAGRATION** | fires **RAZING** | It's so **EXHILARATING**, exciting, **INVIGORATING** | Inviting and **STIMULATING** | I don't ever want to go | It's so **INDISPUTABLE** what this jam will do to you | It's certain you gonna like it from your **FOLLICLES** to cuticles | Whenever we perform, this song they want it | **MARQUEE** above the entrance got our name on it | It's got flames on it, opposite of being **FRIGID** | If you're frozen or under the **TUNDRA** come get with it | It'll thaw you out in a New York minute | Soon as we **DECREE** for the DJ to spin it | Got it on blast | **PERPETUATE** the party yeah we wanna make it last | **INDEFATIGABLE** crowd | No they never get tired | Like

they drunk a hundred cups of coffee all stay wired | Hot enough to cause a riot, someone go and get a hose | We gonna soak you up with water that'll **SATURATE** your clothes | **DEVOID** of **UNIFORMITY** not the same old song | Not **MONOTONOUS** the hotness is gonna blaze on, Yeah. | It's blazing hot in here | Hot | Temperature's changing | Hot | **IGNITED** and flaming | Hot | There's no mistaking | **CONFLAGRATION**, fires **RAZING** | It's so **EXHILARATING**, exciting, **INVIGORATING** | Inviting and **STIMULATING**, I don't ever want to go | So hot in here, make me want to sing | Oo, oo, ooo | So hot in here, make me want to sing | Oo, oo, ooo | So hot in here, make me want to sing | Oo, oo, ooo | So hot in here, make me want to sing

dic•tion•ar•y

Conflagration (n)—inferno, fire.
> *During the summer, when the weather is hot and dry, brushland in the Western United States is often beset by conflagrations.*

Decree (n)—proclamation, ruling, declaration; an official statement that something must happen.
> *The king issued a decree stating that his birthday would be a holiday.*

Devoid (adj)—lacking, deficient, without. Antonym: plentiful (adj).
> *Amish homes are devoid of appliances because their faith forbids the use of electricity.*

Exhilarating (adj)—thrilling, elating. Antonym: boring (adj).
> *Sky diving is exhilarating.*

Fluctuation (n)—flux, variation; a state of varying irregularly; rise and fall. Antonym: stability (n).
> *Fluctuations in the temperature have made it hard to get to the beach this summer; one day it's hot, the next day it's frigid.*

Follicle (n)—small hole present in skin; the best known are those though which hair grows, "hair follicles."
> *He went bald, so he bought a formula that claims to revitalize your hair follicles.*

Frigid (adj)—freezing, cold. Antonym: hot (adj).
To avoid New York's frigid winters, she resides in Florida during January and February.

Frustrating (v)—exasperating, vexing, annoying. Antonym: soothing (v).
It's frustrating to find a long line at the cafeteria when I'm hungry.

Fusion (n)—synthesis; the blending or joining together as a whole. Antonym: separation (n).
The mad scientist's fusion of an elephant with a kangaroo created a "kangaphant."

Ignite (v)—1. light, kindle. Antonym: extinguish (v).
She used a lighter to ignite the firewood.

Ignite (v)—2. to initiate an angry or controversial situation. Antonym: pacify (v).
Tensions were ignited when the protesters' petition was rejected by the city.

Illusion (n)—delusion, chimera; false notion; figment of one's imagination. Antonym: reality (n).
To create the illusion of being sawed in half, the magician's assistant curls up in one of the boxes before the magician separates them.

Indefatigable (adj)—unrelenting, tireless, determined; never willing to admit defeat.
She is an indefatigable supporter of education reform and tirelessly lobbies the government.

Indisputable (adj)—unquestionable, certain. Antonym: disputable (adj).
It is indisputable that the Yankees have won more championships than any other team in baseball.

Invigorating (adj)—revitalizing, energizing. Antonym: draining (adj).
He was refreshed after he went for an invigorating run in the park.

Marquee (n)—canopy above an entrance; a shelter above a theater entrance.
When it began to rain, she ran for shelter under the theater marquee.

Monotony (n)—repetitiveness, sameness. Antonym: variety (n).
Sometimes the monotony of long drives makes me tired.

Perpetuate (v)—preserve, continue, maintain; make something last. Antonym: terminate (v).
The local preservation society is working to perpetuate the community's history.

Perusing (v)—scrutinizing, examining; to read with care. Antonym: skim (v).
She spends her entire Sunday perusing the newspaper for interesting articles.

Profusion (n)—overabundance, excess, surplus, many; large amount. Antonym: dearth (n).
International copyright laws are being revised to stem the profusion of counterfeit goods.

Propagate (v)—reproduce, spread. Antonym: confine (v).
Scientists working with endangered giant pandas are encouraging them to breed in order to propagate the species.

Proximity (n)—nearness, closeness in relation, immediacy. Antonym: distance (n).
We can walk to the movie theater instead of driving there because of its close proximity to the house.

Pursuing (v)—following, chasing; to go after something.
He's pursuing a career in acting so of course he moved to Hollywood.

Raze (v)—level, burn, devastate, destroy; tear down. Antonym: build (v).
The conflagration razed the town.

Rectify (v)—repair, fix; to correct or resolve a problem.
The power plant's staff met to determine how they would rectify the blackout.

Remedy (n)—cure, medicine.
The best remedy for a broken heart is to find solace in your friends.

Saturate (v)—soak, drench. Antonym: dry (v).
Coming in from a long jog, her uniform was saturated with sweat.

Seclusion (n)—isolation, privacy, solitude. Antonym: company (n).
The actress went into seclusion to avoid the press.

Sedentary (adj)—inactive. Antonym: active (adj).
His doctor told him to modify his sedentary lifestyle by getting off of the couch and joining a gym.

Stimulating (adj)—inspiring; thought provoking. Antonym: dull (adj).
She found their conversation about the upcoming election stimulating.

Tundra (n)—rolling, treeless plain in the North American arctic and Siberia.
My parents went to Alaska to watch caribou roaming the tundra.

Ungainly (adj)—awkward, clumsy, ungraceful. Antonym: graceful (adj).
Penguins walk in an ungainly manner on land; however, they swim gracefully through the water.

Uniformity (n)—standardization, regularity, consistency. Antonym: irregularity (n).
Restaurant chains strive to maintain the uniformity of their food at all of their locations.

Union (n)—combination, amalgamation, merger. Antonym: separation (n).
At my aunt's wedding the justice of the peace asked, "Is there anyone who objects to this union?"

Vacillate (v)—waver, fluctuate. Antonym: decide (v).
They couldn't make up their minds and vacillated between getting a cat or a dog.

Wavering (v)—hesitating, faltering; inability to decide or focus. Antonym: deciding (v).
The mayor rebuked wavering council members for their hesitancy to support his position.

"It's **frustrating** always being compared to Britney because we are two very different artists."—*Christina Aguilera*

SYNONYM MATCHI♫G

Match the following words with their synonyms. Note the letter of the matching synonym in the space adjacent to the word.

_____ Conflagration

_____ Decree

_____ Devoid   _____ Profusion

_____ Exhilarating   _____ Propagate

_____ Fluctuation   _____ Proximity

_____ Follicles   _____ Pursue

_____ Frigid   _____ Raze

_____ Frustrating   _____ Rectify

_____ Fusion   _____ Remedy

_____ Ignite   _____ Saturate

_____ Illusion   _____ Seclusion

_____ Indefatigable   _____ Sedentary

_____ Indisputable   _____ Stimulate

_____ Invigorating   _____ Tundra

_____ Marquee   _____ Ungainly

_____ Monotony   _____ Uniformity

_____ Perpetuate   _____ Union

_____ Peruse   _____ Vacillation

                      _____ Waver

(a) arctic plain
(b) spread
(c) standardization
(d) cold
(e) awkward
(f) continue
(g) kindle
(h) repetitiveness
(i) follow
(j) inspire
(k) soak
(l) fire
(m) excess
(n) hesitate
(o) inactive
(p) correct
(q) holes in skin
(r) isolation
(s) variation
(t) join
(u) unrelenting
(v) delusion
(w) indecision
(x) revitalizing
(y) declaration
(z) level
(a1) thrilling
(a2) lacking
(a3) canopy
(a4) annoying
(a5) certain
(a6) scrutinize
(a7) combination
(a8) nearness
(a9) cure

sentencecompl@tion

Using a form or tense of the words below, find the one to best complete each of the following sentences.

WORD BANK

Conflagration	Ignited	Profusion	Sedentary
Decree	Illusion	Propagate	Stimulating
Devoid	Indefatigable	Proximity	Tundra
Exhilarating	Indisputable	Pursuing	Ungainly
Fluctuation	Invigorating	Raze	Uniformity
Follicles	Marquee	Rectify	Union
Frigid	Monotony	Remedy	Vacillate
Frustrating	Perpetuate	Saturate	Wavering
Fusion	Perusing	Seclusion	

1. During the debate, his opponent found his remarks to be _____ , making it difficult for him to debate against him.

2. He is following his dream by _____ a career in law.

3. An open, rolling plain, there is little vegetation on the _____ .

4. Her _____ were damaged over the years by the constant dying and straightening of her hair.

5. The _____ that razed the forest is thought to have been started by a cigarette.

6. The presidential candidates are _____ their ideas by making speeches throughout the country.

7. She was _____ by her little brother's refusal to move his feet off of her books.

8. My backpack was _____ because it had too many books in it.

9. The Olympic torch was _____ during the opening ceremony in Athens.

10. The _____ declared that the country would be handed over to its new government.

11. She enjoys the college classes that she's taking, and she finds them very _____ .

12. Her income is never steady; it usually _____ between $40,000 and $100,000 a year.

13. It's as though he's an immovable, _____ blob; he's always vegging out in front of the television.

14. We have to get that boy out of the house; he'd find my new morning exercise program _____ .

15. The numbing _____ of her life bored her, eventually leading her to quit her job to travel around the world.

16. Working to figure out what was wrong, the technicians were doing everything they could to _____ the problem.

17. My grandmother believes that the best _____ for a cold is homemade chicken soup.

18. His plan to ride a ferret across the country defies logic and is _____ of any sense.

19. She is an _____ competitor who gives 100 percent of herself during every game.

20. In some cultures women are kept in _____ and are rarely seen in public.

21. While I'm editing the book, I need to _____ the exercises to verify that everything makes sense.

22. Alaska isn't always _____ ; as a matter of fact, during the summer it can get quite hot.

23. The building's manager decided to replace the _____ over the main entrance.

24. The best thing about the location of my office is its _____ to my house.

25. The studio released its latest movie and inundated the press with a _____ of PR materials.

26. I've heard that hang gliding is _____ and that there is no thrill that can compare.

27. At the end of the day, I'm tired and my concentration tends to _____ .

28. His music is described as a _____ of hip hop and alternative styles.

29. The novel *1984* is a cautionary tale that describes the monotony of a society based on _____ .

30. The aim of a preservation society is to _____ the culture and traditions of its country.

31. She is _____ between taking a job that is closer to home and a job that offers more money.

32. The next door neighbors _____ their house and are building an entirely new one on the same foundation.

33. The massive corporate merger is reported to be a _____ of equals.

34. Mirages are only _____ caused by the heat rising off of the desert sand, which distorts the view of the horizon.

35. The tie-dying instructions require you to _____ the shirt with water before you place it in the dye.

SYNONYM SENTENCES

In these sentences, use a form or tense of the words below to match their **bolded** synonyms, and write your choice in the space provided following each sentence.

Conflagration	Ignited	Profusion	Sedentary
Decree	Illusion	Propagate	Stimulating
Devoid	Indefatigable	Proximity	Tundra
Exhilarating	Indisputable	Pursuing	Ungainly
Fluctuation	Invigorating	Raze	Uniformity
Follicles	Marquee	Rectify	Union
Frigid	Monotony	Remedy	Vacillate
Frustrating	Perpetuate	Saturate	Wavering
Fusion	Perusing	Seclusion	

WORD BANK

1. Stock prices **vary** day to day. _____

2. During the long winters the **arctic plain** is barren and cold. _____

3. The **fire** spread quickly, but thankfully, no one was hurt. _____

4. I enjoy reading the newspaper because I find it **thought-provoking**. _____

11

5. Her mother always said, "**Follow** your dreams." _____

6. He **lit** the campfire with a match. _____

7. "We will do whatever is necessary to **correct** the situation." _____

8. The researcher **scrutinized** the results of the study prior to making any announcements regarding its outcome. _____

9. She was an **unrelenting** protester against animal testing and didn't end her boycott until the company agreed to release its monkeys. _____

10. When he does his homework, he likes to **isolate** himself. _____

11. She had made her dream come true; her name was in lights on the theater **canopy**. _____

12. It isn't always easy making choices and sometimes I **am uncertain**. _____

13. I'm not sure that those dance lessons are helping him out very much; he still looks **awkward** when he does his routine. _____

14. I find it **exasperating** when people jostle me to get into the subway. _____

15. This summer she has a job in a factory, putting popsicle sticks in molds all day, and she said that the **repetition** is going to drive her crazy. _____

16. As a result of his **less-than-active** lifestyle, he was 50 pounds overweight. _____

17. A native of southern California, he finds Massachusetts **cold**. _____

18. The best **cure** for the flu is to drink lots of fluids and to get some rest. _____

19. He **hesitated** before asking her out on a date. _____

20. The community group was the result of a **combination** of different factions from throughout the area. _____

21. When manufacturing consumer goods, it is important to have a measure of **standardization** to ensure that each item produced is the same. _____

22. Despite the **overabundance** of TV channels, I can never find anything to watch. _____

23. My dad says, "Of course you can't find anything good on, TV is **lacking** of anything intellectually stimulating." _____

24. Our parents bought our house based on its **being close** to a good school. _____

25. He was traumatized at the circus when he was a kid, so he now lives in **continual** fear of little dogs riding bicycles. _____

26. After the hurricane severely damaged the house, we needed to **level** it and build a new one. _____

27. The defendant's lawyer stated, "Given the facts of the case, it is **unquestionable** that my client is innocent." _____

28. The special-interest group worked to **spread** rumors about the competing candidate. _____

29. The sponge won't hold any more liquid—it's **soaked**. _____

30. We went to an interesting restaurant last night where the cuisine was a **blend** of Cuban and Chinese foods. _____

31. Four-foot-three inches tall and 90 pounds, he had no **delusions** that he was going to win a round against the boxing champ. _____

32. My visit to the day spa was **revitalizing**. _____

33. My friend said that bungee jumping in New Zealand was **thrilling**, although I'm not sure that I'd want to try it. _____

34. The crazy king issued a **proclamation** stating that all of the country's citizens were required to wear their socks on the outside of their shoes. _____

35. If you look closely at your arm, you can see the **holes** in your skin. _____

ᴛʜᴇ ARTICLE

Read the following article and then, for each question, select the one statement that best describes the author's remarks.

MIDDLETON AND WILLIE, TOO "HOT"

Brooklyn—Keith Middleton and Rodney Willie are two of the most exhilarating artists we've worked with. Igniting the scene with their profusion of beats and indisputable rhymes, they fuse music from around the world in a conflagration of genius and decree it their own.

I also need to acknowledge the indefatigable and stimulating Avon Marshall, who sang the lead on this track. Devoid of any of the self-consciousness that becomes so ungainly in a vocal booth, his talent is no illusion. Even as the temperature in the studio fluctuated, he stayed true.

Their music shatters the monotony that saturates the airwaves today, razing the state of uniformity that is so perpetually frustrating. Invigorating and a remedy to rectify the soul, it's impossible for me to be sedentary when I'm listening to their tracks.

Successfully pursuing their music careers and propagating their reputations, you'll see their names on a marquee or when you're perusing the bins for CDs. Having worked in close proximity to them, I can tell you that they are the perfect union of talents, and there is no vacillating on this, with Rodney's mile-long dreds, his follicles are ready for prime time. Far from seeking seclusion on the frigid tundra, these boys aren't wavering; they're making it happen.—*Keith London*

Question 1

(a) Keith Middleton and Rodney Willie are exhilarated.
(b) The author enjoys working with Rodney and Keith.
(c) Keith and Rodney get excited when they work with fire.
(d) The artists are exhilarated to work with the author.

Question 2

(a) The artists utilize fire as a metaphor for their music.
(b) Rodney Willie and Keith Middleton are pyromaniacs.
(c) The author is using fire as a metaphor to describe the intensity of the artists' music.
(d) Keith and Rodney use too many beats and rhymes that you cannot question.

Question 3

(a) The artists combine different musical styles to create a unique sound.
(b) The author witnessed the artists using a blast furnace to forge new music.
(c) Rodney and Keith combine different musical genres by starting conflagrations.
(d) Keith Middleton and Rodney Willie are in a position to issue official declarations.

Question 4

(a) Avon is a tireless and inspiring performer.
(b) Avon leads Rodney Willie and Keith Middleton.
(c) The singer who provides the lead vocal track for "Hot" is never willing to admit defeat.
(d) The singer who provides the lead vocal track for "Hot" is unrelenting and thought-provoking.

Question 5

(a) Avon does not use thaumaturgy to enhance his performances.
(b) The singer's awkwardness in the recording session indicated a lack of any discernible talent.
(c) The changes in the production studio's temperature caused Avon to be candid.
(d) Avon Marshall is a genuinely gifted performer and is very comfortable in the studio.

Question 6

(a) Keith and Rodney are drenched by sameness.
(b) Keith and Rodney write music that mixes it up.
(c) Keith and Rodney write music that breaks glass.
(d) Keith and Rodney compose music that is on par with other performers you hear on the radio today.

Question 7

(a) The artists' music forges its own path, breaking the typical boundaries present in today's playlists.
(b) The author is exasperated by the artists' music causing fires in places where standard-ization is the rule.
(c) The artists are continually vexed by the devastation caused by today's radios.
(d) Rodney and Keith want to encourage standardization and seek to preserve their exasperation.

Question 8

(a) The author finds the artists' music energizing and believes that it can be used to cure illnesses.
(b) The author finds the artists energized.
(c) The artists want to be seated, but the author is insisting that they get up.
(d) The author finds the artists' music energizing and regards it as a metaphorical cure for one's state of well-being.

Question 9

(a) Rodney and Keith are spreading their music and following their reputations.
(b) The artists are making it in the music industry and are building their reputations.
(c) Keith and Rodney are following a career in music and are looking to reproduce their reputations.
(d) The author feels that the artists are followers working to spread their reputation.

Question 10

(a) The author expects the artists to perform publicly, sell their CDs in stores, and become famous.
(b) The author expects the artists to put their names on a canopy and anticipates that readers will scrutinize their CDs.
(c) The artists anticipate that you will soon be shopping for CDs.
(d) None of the above

Question 11

(a) Rodney and Keith work too closely together and won't make any decisions.
(b) Rodney's hair is very long and consequently, his follicles belong on TV.
(c) The artists and author have worked closely, giving the author an appreciation for the artists' talents and their preparedness for stardom.
(d) The artists have worked closely with the author and have expressed a predisposition for prime-time television.

Question 12

(a) Keith and Rodney are looking forward to their trip to Alaska.
(b) Rodney and Keith are working hard to achieve stardom.
(c) The artists aren't hesitant in their ambition to visit the tundra.
(d) All of the above

ALREADY TAKEN

Listening Exercise

Listen to "Already Taken" all the way through at least once. Then listen to the song again, and graffiti up the wall with the new or unfamiliar words that you hear. Don't worry if you don't fill up the whole wall . . . it won't be that deleterious . . .

ALREADY TAKEN | Mia Johnson of The Mia Johnson Band | Lyrics by Mia Johnson | Music Written & Performed by Mia Johnson & The Mia Johnson Band | Guitar & Vocals: Mia Johnson | Guitar: Rocco DeCicco | Bass Guitar: Jeff Hiatt | Drums: Tom Walling | Produced by Dave Logan & Craig Chang

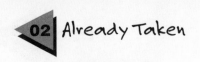

LYRICS

| You are standing next to me | And at this **PROXIMITY** | You are **DELETERIOUS** | To my **TRANQUILITY** | I catch a whiff of your **AROMA** | That is so **INIMITABLY** you | And the **DELIRIUM** that follows | Is **TORTUOUS** pure **ECSTASY** | Cuz you are so off-limits | And I am really just not kidding | I repeat this like an **INCANTATION** | Cuz I see you **INEVITABLY** each day | No matter how **ENAMORED** I am of you | It cannot change a thing in this world | Because you are, already taken by my best friend | They've been together for three years | A **CONSUMMATE** and **INTERMINABLE** pairing | But now **CONVERSELY** their love appears | To be a **SENESCENT** habit they're sharing | And I **INTUIT** your attraction to me | That you **LABORIOUSLY SHROUD** | And we keep our **RETICENCE SYNCHRONOUSLY** | Because it's perfectly **FUTILE** to say it out loud | Cuz you are so off-limits | And I am really just not kidding | I repeat this like an **INCANTATION** | Cuz I see you **INEVITABLY** each day | No matter how **ENAMORED** I am of you | It cannot change a thing in this world | Because you are, already taken by my best friend | And this **AMOROUS** way I feel about you now | Could just be | Some undue **INFATUATION** | Just not worth losing my best friend, to me | So I simply have to learn how to **ACQUIESCE** in | This **AWKWARD SITUATION** | Cuz you are so off-limits | And I am really just not kidding | I repeat this like an **INCANTATION** | Cuz I see you **INEVITABLY** each day | No matter how **ENAMORED** I am of you | It cannot change a thing in this world | Cuz you are already taken | Yeah you are already taken | Yeah you are already taken

dic•tion•ar•y

Acquiesce (v)—assent; agree without protest. Antonym: protest (v), resist (v).
Despite his reservations, he knew he would have to acquiesce to his boss' demands.

Amorous (adj)—affectionate; related to love or romance. Antonym: hateful (adj).
The lovers amorously gazed at one another.

Aroma (n)—fragrant, pleasing scent. Antonym: stench (n).
The aroma of her perfume was sweet and exotic.

Awkward (adj)—1. to be uncomfortable in a situation. Antonym: relaxed (adj).
It was awkward to see my best friend at the mall with my older brother.

Awkward (adj)—2. clumsy; difficult to handle. Antonym: graceful (adj).
The clown's giant shoes caused him to walk awkwardly.

Consummate (adj)—archetypal, standard, picture-perfect.
A skilled cook and decorator, he is the consummate homemaker.

Conversely (adv)—opposite; contrary. Antonym: analogously (adv).
If he passes the final, he'll receive a B in algebra; conversely, if he fails the final, he'll receive a D.

Deleterious (adj)—harmful, damaging. Antonym: helpful (adj).
Smoking is deleterious to your health.

Delirium (n)—confusion, disorientation. Antonym: clarity (n).
She was in a state of delirium after meeting her favorite movie star.

Ecstasy (n)—rapture, joy, happiness. Antonym: despair (n).
He was ecstatic when he won a trip to the Bahamas.

Enamored (v)—smitten; in love with; also idiomatically used in reference to appreciation for an object. Antonym: repelled (v).
Enamored with the dress, she decided to buy it for the prom.

Futile (adj)—useless, hopeless, pointless. Antonym: useful (adj).
It would be futile to engage Superman in an arm wrestling contest.

Incantation (n)—chant; singing magic spells.
The witch's incantation turned him into a toad.

Inevitably (adv)—certainly, unavoidably.
It was inevitable that airlines would lose business after they raised airfares dramatically.

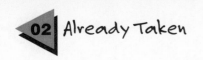

Infatuation (n)—fixation, obsession; an engrossing passion. Antonym: indifference (n).
The stalker was infatuated with the movie star.

Inimitably (adv)—uniquely, distinctly; not able to be imitated.
Inimitably, Snoop Dogg has a style all his own.

Interminable (adj)—endless, incessant. Antonym: finite (adj).
Although the lame movie was short, it seemed interminable to the audience.

Intuit (v)—perceive, infer; know without logic.
I can usually intuit when someone is not telling me the truth.

Laboriously (adv)—painstakingly, tediously, gruelingly; demanding a great deal of work or care. Antonym: easily (adv).
The designer laboriously hand-stitched pearls onto the dress.

Proximity (n)—nearness; closeness in relation. Antonym: distance (n).
When driving, you need to judge the proximity of surrounding cars.

Reticence (n)—reluctance, unwillingness; silence. Antonym: willingness (n).
Being very shy, she showed reticence to voice her opinion during the class discussion.

Senescent (adj)—aging; decaying over time. Antonym: youthful (adj).
The twelve-year-old dog was senescent.

Shroud (n)—1. blanket, veil, cover; a draped material that envelops an object.
At the funeral the widow wore a shroud that veiled her face.

Shroud (v)—2. hide, cover; shield from view. Antonym: uncover (v).
The leaves shrouded the driveway, making it difficult to see the garage.

Situation (n)—predicament; circumstances at a given moment; a state of affairs.
Prior to arresting the protester, the police officer assessed the situation.

Synchronously (adv)—simultaneously, concurrently. Antonym: sequentially (adv).
My favorite TV shows air synchronously, which forces me to miss one.

Tortuous (adj)—1. arduous, trying, difficult. Antonym: easy (adj).
Immigrants find that applying for a green card is a tortuous process.

Tranquility (n)—peacefulness; calm. Antonym: chaos (n).
The tranquility of the Adirondack mountains makes them a great place to spend the summer.

SYNONYM MATCHI♪♪G

Match the following words with their synonyms. Note the letter of the matching synonym in the space adjacent to the word.

_____ Acquiesce

_____ Amorous

_____ Aroma

_____ Awkward

_____ Consummate

_____ Conversely

_____ Deleterious

_____ Delirium

_____ Ecstasy

_____ Enamored

_____ Futile

_____ Incantation

_____ Inevitably

_____ Infatuation

_____ Inimitable

_____ Interminable

_____ Intuit

_____ Laboriously

_____ Proximity

_____ Reticence

_____ Senescent

_____ Shrouded

_____ Situation

_____ Synchronously

_____ Tortuous

_____ Tranquility

(a)	arduous
(b)	spell
(c)	endless
(d)	certainly
(e)	contrary
(f)	simultaneously
(g)	agree
(h)	predicament
(i)	perceive
(j)	joy
(k)	pleasing scent
(l)	nearness
(m)	covered
(n)	archetypal
(o)	smitten
(p)	peacefulness
(q)	aging
(r)	uncomfortable
(s)	fixation
(t)	unique
(u)	affectionate
(v)	gruelingly
(w)	reluctance
(x)	useless
(y)	harmful
(z)	disorientation

sentencecompletion

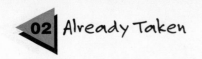

Using a form or tense of the words below, find the one to best complete each of the following sentences.

WORD BANK

Acquiesce	Enamored	Proximity
Amorous	Futile	Reticence
Aroma	Incantation	Senescent
Awkward	Inevitably	Shroud
Consummate	Infatuation	Situation
Conversely	Inimitable	Synchronously
Deleterious	Interminable	Tortuous
Delirium	Intuit	Tranquility
Ecstasy	Laborious	

1. We live in close _____ to our neighbors.

2. Time never stops and _____ , everything changes.

3. She was in a state of _____ when she was accepted to Yale.

4. In the United States people drive on the right-hand side of the road; _____ , in Britain you would drive on the left-hand side.

5. The hikers' route through the mountain pass was _____ .

6. When the boxer regained consciousness after getting knocked out, he awoke in a state of _____ .

7. The president of the student government _____ to the demands of the student body.

8. Professionals working in the fashion industry strive to create their own _____ style.

9. His father's stories about his childhood were _____ .

10. Given the fact that she can't sing, it's _____ for her to try out for *American Idol,* unless she wants to be on the blooper episode!

11. The hood of the explorer's parka _____ her face.

12. My mother became _____ with my father the first time she saw him.

13. I love the _____ of the ocean when the weather is calm.

14. She could _____ that I was worried about my upcoming exam.

15. Feeding a dog chocolate can be _____ to its health.

16. She was _____ with her favorite band, and she listened to their CD constantly.

17. The _____ of freshly baked pastries filled the air.

18. She created an awkward _____ by asking me to help her cheat on the test.

19. It was _____ for me to see my dad dating after my parents got divorced.

20. The witches chanted an _____ around a boiling potion.

21. A _____ professional, she managed the meeting flawlessly.

22. After the banquet, he _____ washed every dish by hand.

23. She was _____ to speak in front of the class.

24. On some SUVs the front wheels move _____ with the back wheels.

25. The 14-year-old cat is _____ .

26. The two lovers gazed at one another _____ .

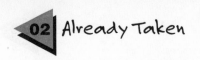

SYNONYM SENTENCES

In these sentences, use a form or tense of the words below to match their **bolded** synonyms, and write your choice in the space provided following each sentence.

Acquiesce	Enamored	Proximity
Amorous	Futile	Reticence
Aroma	Incantation	Senescent
Awkward	Inevitably	Shroud
Consummate	Infatuation	Situation
Conversely	Inimitable	Synchronously
Deleterious	Interminable	Tortuous
Delirium	Intuit	Tranquility
Ecstasy	Laborious	

1. The bakery was filled with the **scent** of fresh bread. _____

2. If you don't have a CD player, it's **useless** to try to listen to a CD. _____

3. She discovered an **affectionate** love letter in her locker. _____

4. The sorceress' **spell** made him fall in love with a chicken. _____

5. Her style is **unique**. _____

24

6. The **predicament** she found herself in was unsettling. _____

7. When two things occur at the same time, they happen **simultaneously**. _____

8. She was **elated** when she found out that she had won the Nobel Prize. _____

9. Although she didn't tell him, he could **perceive** when she was mad at him. _____

10. Although my workout is only an hour long, it seems **endless**. _____

11. I am **obsessed** with romantic novels. _____

12. He **agreed** to their demands. _____

13. I am not **in love** with BMW's new designs. _____

14. Polished and poised, she was the **picture-perfect** professional. _____

15. They were the consummate odd couple; she was outgoing, and **in contrast**, he was shy. _____

16. The bus was in such **close relation** to my car that it almost hit us. _____

17. After the accident, the driver was in a state of **confusion**. _____

18. When going on a first date, I always feel **uncomfortable**. _____

19. Shaking a baby can be **harmful** to the child's health. _____

20. I enjoy the **peacefulness** of a quiet afternoon. _____

21. It is **unavoidable** that children will grow up. _____

22. The old crumbling building is **decaying**. _____

23. He was **reluctant** to share his opinions with the class. _____

24. Often, the path to success is **arduous**. _____

25. The first snowfall of winter **covered** the hills. _____

26. Writing a novel by hand is a **grueling** task. _____

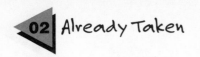

ARTICLE

Read the following article and then, for each question, select the one statement that best describes the authors' remarks.

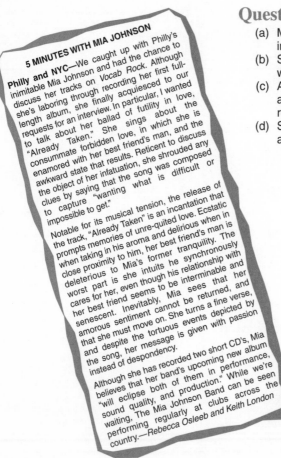

5 MINUTES WITH MIA JOHNSON

Philly and NYC—We caught up with Philly's inimitable Mia Johnson and had the chance to discuss her tracks on *Vocab Rock*. Although she's laboring through recording her first full-length album, she finally acquiesced to our requests for an interview. In particular, I wanted to talk about her ballad of futility in love, "Already Taken." She sings about the consummate forbidden love, in which she is enamored with her best friend's man, and the awkward state that results. Reticent to discuss the object of her infatuation, she shrouded any clues by saying that the song was composed to capture "wanting what is difficult or impossible to get."

Notable for its musical tension, the release of the track, "Already Taken" is an incantation that prompts memories of unre-quited love. Ecstatic when taking in his aroma and delirious when in close proximity to him, her best friend's man is deleterious to Mia's former tranquility. The worst part is she intuits he synchronously cares for her, even though his relationship with her best friend seems to be interminable and senescent. Inevitably, Mia sees that her amorous sentiment cannot be returned, and that she must move on. She turns a fine verse, and despite the tortuous events depicted by the song, her message is given with passion instead of despondency.

Although she has recorded two short CD's, Mia believes that her band's upcoming new album "will eclipse both of them in performance, sound quality, and production." While we're waiting, The Mia Johnson Band can be seen performing regularly at clubs across the country.—*Rebecca Osleeb and Keith London*

Question 1

(a) Mia had plenty of time for the interview.
(b) She easily agreed to speak with the authors.
(c) After many requests, Mia agreed to do the interview with resignation.
(d) She was happy to take time away from her other projects.

Question 2

(a) Her current project is easy.
(b) Recording a full-length CD is grueling work.
(c) Recording a full-length CD is a tranquil experience.
(d) She wasn't occupied with any work other than recording "Already Taken."

Question 3

(a) Mia isn't unique.
(b) Her style is widely copied and indistinguishable from other performers.
(c) She wants to leave Philadelphia.
(d) Mia has her own unique style.

Question 4

(a) She believes that love is readily attainable.
(b) Mia's song expresses the idea that there is "someone for everyone."
(c) "Already Taken" is a song about someone having stolen Mia's car.
(d) Mia sings about the difficulty of falling for someone who cannot reciprocate.

Question 5

(a) Mia is going to resign from her friendship.
(b) She acknowledges that she can't date her best friend's boyfriend.
(c) She recognized her love of sediment and will hire a mover to bring it back.
(d) Mia decided to move out of her apartment.

Question 6

(a) Mia hates her best friend's boyfriend.
(b) She has no problem managing her situation.
(c) Her predicament has left her feeling uncomfortable.
(d) "Already Taken" describes how easy it can be to eat your best friend's lunch.

Question 7

(a) She did not readily discuss about whom she may have written the song.
(b) Mia was happy to tell the authors about the subject of her infatuation.
(c) The authors easily recognized the relationship that inspired the song.
(d) The song's lyrics are about things that are easily obtained.

Question 8

(a) Mia sings slowly.
(b) Her song only has one defining characteristic.
(c) "Already Taken" uses music to give the listener contrasting feelings.
(d) She wrote the music to soothe the listener.

Question 9

(a) "Already Taken" is like a mystical chant that causes the listener to remember.
(b) Mia is a witch.
(c) The authors can't remember anything.
(d) Her songs bring back memories of old friends.

Question 10

(a) Mia's lyrics describe how much she dislikes her best friend's boyfriend.
(b) Her girlfriend's boyfriend lives near her house.
(c) She sings about how badly her best friend's boyfriend smells.
(d) Mia is obsessed with her girlfriend's boyfriend and the situation is awkward.

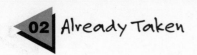

Question 11

(a) The boyfriend secretly likes her but can't break up with her friend.
(b) "Already Taken" describes a friendship that never ends.
(c) Mia needs to synchronize her watch.
(d) Her best friend has an odd scent.

Question 12

(a) The events discussed in "Already Taken" are readily resolved.
(b) Mia's storytelling reflects vitality rather than sadness.
(c) She's a depressing writer.
(d) Her song causes the listener to turn around.

I'm in **ecstasy** over all these rockin' new words . . .

SHINE

Listening Exercise

Listen to "Shine" all the way through at least once. Then listen to the song again, and graffiti up the wall with the new or unfamiliar words that you hear. Don't worry if you don't fill up the whole wall . . .we won't scoff at you . . .

SHINE | Joe Pascarell & The Machine | Lyrics by Joe Pascarell | Music Written & Performed by Joe Pascarell & The Machine | Guitar: Joe Pascarell | Bass Guitar & Vocals: Ryan Ball | Drums: Todd Cohen | Produced by Joe Pascarell

LYRICS

| I feel **ACTUATED** | I push through the **WELTER** of my life | Done with **VACILLATION** | I am **RABID** in my aim | No more **LURKING** | Watch me | I will shine | **ILLUMINATE** me | Don't **FORSAKE** me | I am **RESPLENDENT** in the day | **SCOFF** at all that's in my way | **CAPTIVATED** by this life | I will shine | | Living in **SECLUSION** | Taking **SOLACE** in my pain | Feeling like a **MARTYR** | I was **MIRED** in the **DREGS** | No more **SKULKING** | Watch me | I will shine | **RENOVATE** me | Don't **FORSAKE** me | I am **RESPLENDENT** in the day | **SCOFF** at all that's in my way | **CAPTIVATED** by this life | Hold the fire inside | That's **INCITING** me to shine | **ILLUMINATE** me | Don't **FORSAKE** me | I am **RESPLENDENT** in the day | **SCOFF** at all that's in my way | **CAPTIVATED** by this life | Hold the fire inside | I am **RESPLENDENT** in the day | **SCOFF** at all that's in my way | **CAPTIVATED** by this life | Hold the fire inside that's **INCITING** me to shine | I am **RESPLENDENT** in the day | **SCOFF** at all that's in my way | **CAPTIVATED** by this life | Hold the fire inside that's **INCITING** me to shine | I am **RESPLENDENT** in the day | **SCOFF** at all that's in my way | **CAPTIVATED** by this life | Hold the fire inside that's **INCITING** me to shine | I am **RESPLENDENT** in the day | **SCOFF** at all that's in my way | **CAPTIVATED** by this life | Hold the fire inside that's **INCITING** me to shine

dic•tion•ar•y

Actuate (v)—motivate; to put into action.
He was actuated by his drive to succeed.

Captivate (v)—entrance, charm, enthrall. Antonym: repel (v).
The audience was captivated by her virtuoso performance.

Dregs (n)—sediment, muck, residue, remains, leftovers; what is left behind.
Finishing the entire bottle of chocolate milk, he drank it down to the dregs.

Forsake (v)—abandon, renounce, desert. Antonym: devote (v).
Religious leaders ask their followers not to forsake their faith.

Illuminate (v)—1. enlighten, clarify; make something understood. Antonym: obfuscate (v).
His novel illuminates the issues preceding the Civil War.

Illuminate (v)—2. brighten. Antonym: darken (v).
The footlights illuminated the stage.

Incite (v)—compel, spur, impel, provoke, goad; to cause. Antonym: soothe (v).
The jury's controversial verdict incited a riot.

Lurk (v)—prowl, hide; lie in wait; move about stealthily or undetected.
He was seen lurking around the parking lot before the truck was stolen.

Martyr (n)—one who is subjugated; one who endures pain or suffers voluntarily typically to incite change. Antonym: oppressor (n).
She fought for women's rights all of her life and died a martyr for the cause.

Mired (adj)—1. caught up; in a difficult situation.
She was mired in the conflict between her parents.

Mired (adj)—2. trapped by a thick substance. Antonym: unhindered (adj).
His shoes became mired in the mud.

Rabid (adj)—1. extreme, fanatical. Antonym: casual (adj).
He was a rabid Yankees fan and never missed a game.

Rabid (adj)—2. infected with rabies.
The dog that bit her was rabid, so she needed a tetanus shot.

Renovate (v)—refurbish, restore. Antonym: demolish (v).
They decided to renovate the 100-year-old house rather than demolish it.

03 Shine

Resplendent (adj)—dazzling, stunning, glorious, brilliant. Antonym: dull (adj).
She was resplendent in her sequined gown.

Scoff (v)—mock, ridicule; make fun of. Antonym: encourage (v).
The critics scoffed at the comic's attempt to play a dramatic role.

Seclusion (n)—isolation, privacy, solitude. Antonym: company (n).
Whenever he was depressed, he avoided his friends and went into seclusion.

Skulk (v)—creep, loiter, sneak; to move furtively or secretly. Antonym: parade (v).
The spy skulked through the city's streets, hoping he wouldn't be detected.

Solace (n)—comfort, support. Antonym: distress (n).
After her husband left her, she found solace in writing.

Vacillation (n)—indecision, uncertainty; inability to decide. Antonym: decision (n).
His vacillation between the candidates was obvious as he endorsed neither one.

Welter (n)—turmoil; bewildering jumble; a confused mass. Antonym: order (n).
A welter of decade-old newspapers is piled in the garage

SYNONYM MATCHI♫G

Match the following words with their synonyms. Note the letter of the matching synonym in the space adjacent to the word.

_____ Actuated

_____ Captivated

_____ Dregs   _____ Rabid

_____ Forsake   _____ Renovate

_____ Illuminate   _____ Resplendent

_____ Incite   _____ Scoff

_____ Lurk   _____ Seclusion

_____ Martyred   _____ Skulk

_____ Mired   _____ Solace

                     _____ Vacillation

                     _____ Welter

(a) abandon
(b) sediment
(c) comfort
(d) isolation
(e) lie-in-wait
(f) dazzling
(g) indecision
(h) caught up
(i) refurbish
(j) sneak
(k) confusion
(l) clarify
(m) charmed
(n) fanatical
(o) motivate
(p) goad
(q) mock
(r) subjugated

sentencecompletion

Using a form or tense of the words below, find the one to best complete each of the following sentences.

WORD BANK

Actuated	Lurking	Scoff
Captivated	Martyr	Seclusion
Dregs	Mired	Skulking
Forsake	Rabid	Solace
Illuminate	Renovate	Vacillation
Inciting	Resplendent	Welter

1. Her children tried to give her _____ following her husband's tragic death.

2. The demonstrator was overrun by government forces and died a _____ for his cause.

3. Paparazzi often _____ in the bushes around celebrities' homes, waiting to ambush them.

4. He was so embarrassed after pouring a drink down the front of his pants that he _____ away from the party.

5. She was bitten by a hamster when she was a child, and she's had a _____ hatred of them ever since.

6. Critics _____ at Henry Ford's early attempts to build a car.

7. He was fired for _____ co-workers to rebel against the new company rules.

8. The story and the beauty of the film _____ audiences around the world.

9. She _____ between going to Florida and going to California.

10. The entire building was _____ after asbestos was found in the walls.

11. Their strong commitment to their community _____ them to volunteer.

12. Despite our differences, I would never _____ my family.

13. The queen wore a _____ jewel-encrusted gown.

14. Seeking _____ , the reclusive star flew to a private island.

15. There was a _____ of CDs and cassettes to look through at the garage sale.

16. The diary she left behind _____ her thinking and clarified why she ran off with the guy who runs the deli.

17. As the horse pulled the wagon, its wheels became _____ in the mud.

18. She drank the chocolate milk down to the _____ .

SYNONYM SENTENCES

In these sentences, use a form or tense of the words below to match their **bolded** synonyms, and write your choice in the space provided following each sentence.

Actuated	Lurking	Scoff
Captivated	Martyr	Seclusion
Dregs	Mired	Skulking
Forsake	Rabid	Solace
Illuminate	Renovate	Vacillation
Inciting	Resplendent	Welter

WORD BANK

1. He decided to **refurbish** the house. _____

2. Her diamond earrings were **dazzling**. _____

3. He **couldn't decide** between having smooth or chunky peanut butter. _____

4. His blue eyes **enthralled** the girls. _____

5. The girls **mocked** his attempt to join the field hockey team. _____

6. The professor **clarified** the themes conveyed in Shakespeare's plays. _____

7. The prisoner was placed in **isolation** after disobeying the warden. _____

8. I found the cat **hiding** in the bushes, stalking the birds. _____

9. In an effort to **motivate** the players, the coach gave an impassioned speech at halftime. _____

10. She found **comfort** in her friends after losing her job. _____

11. I've been **caught up** in work at the studio. _____

12. The escaped convict was found **sneaking** around the city. _____

13. The professor's office was a **confusion** of books, papers, and scientific bric-a-brac. _____

14. We arrived late to the sale, and the earlier shoppers only left behind the **remains** of what the store had to offer. _____

15. She is a **fanatical** basketball fan. _____

16. He was **spurring** the crowd to riot. _____

17. Would you **abandon** your beliefs for money? _____

18. He went to prison for speaking his mind about the government and **subjugated** himself for his beliefs. _____

THE ARTICLE

Read the following article and then, for each question, select the one statement that best describes the author's remarks.

PASCARELL'S DEFINED MIND SHINES

NYC—Although Joe Pascarell has captivated audiences with his band, The Machine, for more than ten years, he has not forsaken his own art, creating the resplendent anthem "Shine." Here is the story of how fans everywhere lucked out into Joe following his melodic muse.

Having started The Machine with Todd Cohen, Joe scoffed at taking a traditional career, but mired in the welter of youth, he vacillated between jobs while his aspirations evolved. He wasn't a martyr or in the dregs, but he wasn't incited by the rabid pursuit of fame and self-orientation that marks many performers, and it took time for his calling to take shape. Alternately a premier auto mechanic (he used to create and work on blown Porsches) and a landscaper, his path couldn't have been less clear. However, fortunately for us, he was still young when his talent made itself apparent to him and others, and people soon sought him out.

Joe was actuated by a love of the music and a desire to share it with audiences, but it took Todd to illuminate Joe's perspective. Their band was different from the ones that many of us were in when we were in school, more capable, more imaginative, tighter. It didn't take long for Todd to ask Joe to dedicate himself fully to making the band work.

With a renovated sense of purpose, Joe invested himself wholly, and the natural comfort he has on stage ceased to lurk in the shadows. Never one to seek seclusion or to skulk, Joe didn't try to find solace in the spotlight the way other artists do; his ease was simply the result of his passion for his craft, whatever the venue. Although he was always immensely grateful for the audience's appreciation of his talents, when he was on stage the world didn't distract him. It was always first and foremost about the music. Ten years later, it still is... "Shine" announces that Joe's focus is as clear as ever and that his best work is still yet to come.—*Keith London*

Question 1

(a) Joe has held audiences as captives.
(b) His performances have enthralled audiences.
(c) He has a 10-year-old machine that captures audiences.
(d) The Machine hasn't captivated audiences.

Question 2

(a) He has abandoned his individual pursuits in deference to the band.
(b) The Machine worked with Defined Mind on "Shine."
(c) "Shine" is the product of Joe's individual creativity.
(d) Joe has been trying to get out of a machine for ten years.

Question 3

- (a) His music dazzles you.
- (b) Joe's national anthem is "Shine."
- (c) He created something that sparkles brilliantly.
- (d) The song "Shine" is a glorious, brilliant declaration.

Question 4

- (a) The career path he chose was not traditional.
- (b) He mocked his career path.
- (c) Todd Cohen ridiculed Joe's career choice.
- (d) His career path was traditional.

Question 5

- (a) Joe was caught in a mire when he was young.
- (b) He is confused.
- (c) His path unclear, he struggled with the confusion of youth.
- (d) When Joe was young, his welter was mired.

Question 6

- (a) Joe moved between jobs while he was finding himself.
- (b) Jobs precluded him from developing his music.
- (c) He aspired to evolve.
- (d) Moving between jobs caused Joe to aspire.

Question 7

- (a) He subjugated himself for a cause.
- (b) His drinking became a problem because he always drank to the dregs.
- (c) Joe found himself in sediment.
- (d) During his period of indecision, he wasn't suffering.

Question 8

- (a) Joe did not want to fanatically chase fame and fortune.
- (b) His motivation was to incite.
- (c) He sought fame, but it took time for it to take shape.
- (d) Joe was rabid and self-oriented.

Question 9

- (a) He was the first mechanic to blow up a Porsche.
- (b) Joe was a great mechanic who worked on Porsches.
- (c) Joe was a mechanic and a landscaper at the same time.
- (d) He was a landscaper who blew up Porsches.

Question 10

- (a) Todd brought Joe some lighting fixtures.
- (b) Joe was an actuary.
- (c) It was dark and Joe asked Todd for additional illumination.
- (d) His motivation was his love of music, and Todd showed him the way.

Question 11

(a) Joe and Todd's band did renovations.
(b) Joe's hiding in the shadows became his trademark.
(c) He didn't seek the limelight, but he was comfortable there.
(d) His isolation caused him to seek the comfort of the spotlight.

Question 12

(a) Joe was immense.
(b) His audience preferred the Grateful Dead.
(c) He was easily distracted on stage.
(d) None of the above

WHY DIDN'T YOU TELL ME

Listening Exercise

Listen to "Why Didn't You Tell Me" all the way through at least once. Then listen to the song again, and graffiti up the wall with the new or unfamiliar words that you hear. Don't worry if you don't fill up the whole wall . . . but you may very well be enticed to do so!

WHY DIDN'T YOU TELL ME | Nina Zeitlin | Lyrics by Nina Zeitlin & Matt Kelly | Music Written by Nina Zeitlin & Matt Kelly | Vocals: Nina Zeitlin | Guitar & Bass Guitar: Joe Mendoza | Instrumentation: Mike Pandolfo | Produced by Mike Pandolfo

LYRICS

| How come I didn't know you'd be so **SENSUAL** | Why didn't you tell me about your **FLAGRANT** style | Maybe you weren't **COGNIZANT** of anything | How can I make you mine for a while (yeah) | Every single guy that I was with before | Was **CRASS** and **CRAVEN** and insecure | I need a man that knows how to **COLLABORATE** | Instead of someone who just makes me **IRATE** | Tell me how to **ENTICE** you | I really like you | I have an **ADDICTION** to your **COMPLICIT** smile | It's like an **AFFLICTION** | With so much **CONVICTION** | I'll tell you a million times that you're mine (yeah) | Sammy thought that he was so **PROFOUND** | But he couldn't **ASSAY** the deepest thing around (yeah) | From the **REVELATION** that I had figured him out | Too **STOLID, SINISTER** and on the way out | Tell me how to **ENTICE** you | I really like you | I have a **CONJECTURE** about your **ALLURING** eyes | It's like an **AFFLICTION** | With so much **CONVICTION** | I'll tell you a million times that you're mine (yeah) | (I said) I said | Tell me how to **DECOY** you | I really enjoy you | I have an **OBSESSION** with your **COMELY** smile | It is my mission | My **PREDISPOSITION** | I have these feelings that I just can't **SURMISE** (yeah) | How come I didn't know you'd be so **SENSUAL** | Why didn't you tell me about your **FLAGRANT** style | Maybe you weren't **COGNIZANT** of anything | How can I make you mine for a while (yeah) | Mine for a while (yeah), mine for a while (yeah) | How can I make you mine for a while (yeah) |

dic•tion•ar•y

Addiction (n)—dependence; a habitual, compulsive need.
When he was younger, he had an addiction to sugar.
Affliction (n)—illness; cause of suffering; burden.
With an affliction such as arthritis, she found it difficult to walk.

Alluring (v)—appealing, tempting.
He found her distinctive attitude alluring and asked her to join him for dinner.

Assay (v)—test, analyze, evaluate, determine.
It was necessary to assay the bracelet to determine its gold content.

Cognizant (adj)—aware of; to know of something. Antonym: ignorant (adj).
His mirrors were not adjusted properly, so he wasn't cognizant that he had hit the cones during his driving test.

Collaborate (v)—cooperate; work together.
She's heard that Jay-Z and Beyonce will collaborate on upcoming albums.

Comely (adj)—attractive; suitable. Antonym: homely (adj).
She was quite comely and he noticed her the moment she entered the room.

Complicit (adj)—having involvement in, complacent regarding, or ignoring the progress of activity that is improper.
She worked at the store and turned the alarm off for her partners-in-crime during the burglary and was therefore arrested for her complicit actions.

Conjecture (v)—opine, guess, contemplate. Antonym: know (v).
We don't know what caused the accident; we can only conjecture.

Conviction (n)—1. strong opinion or belief. Antonym: vacillation (n).
It is his conviction that murderers should face the death penalty.

Conviction (n)—2. a judgment that one is guilty of a crime. Antonym: acquittal (n).
If he is convicted of murder, he may face the death penalty.

Crass (adj)—tactless, rude, gross, unrefined, blundering. Antonym: refined (adj).
She was jealous that he had a girlfriend, so she made crass remarks about her to his friends.

Craven (adj)—cowardly. Antonym: brave (adj).
The private was too craven to face the enemy and rescue his sergeant.

Decoy (v)—1. to bait; to lure.
They used a hitchhiker to decoy him to stop.

Decoy (n)—2. bait; a lure.
Duck hunters are well-known for using decoys.

Entice (v)—persuade, draw, invite.
To entice urban workers to leave the city, suburban employers are offering them higher salaries.

Flagrant (adj)—conspicuous, blatant, brazen. Antonym: modest (adj).
He believes that many television shows promote violence in a flagrant way.

Irate (adj)—angry, incensed, enraged. Antonym: calm (adj).
He worked as a customer service representative and hated when irate customers called to complain.

Obsession (n)—mania, fixation, compulsion; constant thoughts about something or someone.
He has an obsession with cars and owns more than fifty classics.

Predisposition (n)—inclination, leaning, proclivity, propensity; prone to behave or respond in a given manner.
She's never on time; her predisposition is to be late.

Profound (adj)—deep, thoughtful; of significance.
Steven Hawking, arguably the world's smartest man, has had profound insights into the origins of the universe.

Revelation (n)—disclosure, discovery, insight. Antonym: secret (n).
The media made shocking revelations about former President Bill Clinton's affair.

Sensual (adj)—pleasing to the senses.
Graceful and lissome, the model was noted for her sensual style.

Sinister (adj) — threatening, evil, creepy.
Foreboding and sinister, Dracula is a classic horror figure.

Stolid (adj)—dull, impassive, boring. Antonym: stimulating (adj).
Fitting the stereotype, his accounting professor is a straight-laced, stolid guy.

Surmise (v)—deduce, estimate, infer, gather; figure out.
I was able to surmise how big the parking spot was by comparing it to the car that was next to it.

SYNONYM MATCHING

Match the following words with their synonyms. Note the letter of
the matching synonym in the space adjacent to the word.

_____ Addiction

_____ Affliction

_____ Alluring   _____ Decoy

_____ Assay   _____ Entice

_____ Cognizant   _____ Flagrant

_____ Collaborate   _____ Irate

_____ Comely   _____ Obsession

_____ Complicit   _____ Predisposition

_____ Conjecture   _____ Profound

_____ Conviction   _____ Revelation

_____ Crass   _____ Sensual

_____ Craven   _____ Sinister

    _____ Stolid

    _____ Surmise

(a)	appealing
(b)	lure
(c)	propensity
(d)	deduce
(e)	dependence
(f)	opine
(g)	persuade
(h)	cowardly
(i)	illness
(j)	aware
(k)	blatant
(l)	evil
(m)	evaluate
(n)	complacent
(o)	belief
(p)	disclosure
(q)	attractive
(r)	deep
(s)	pleasing
(t)	angry
(u)	rude
(v)	fixation
(w)	dull
(x)	cooperate

sentence**compl@tion**

Using a form or tense of the words below, find the one to best complete each of the following sentences.

WORD BANK

Addiction	Conjecture	Obsession
Affliction	Conviction	Predisposition
Alluring	Crass	Profound
Assay	Craven	Revelation
Cognizant	Decoy	Sensual
Collaborate	Entice	Sinister
Comely	Flagrant	Stolid
Complicit	Irate	Surmise

1. The beautiful Corvette was a _____ to lure customers into the used-car lot.

2. Her argument with the store manager caused the woman to become _____ .

3. The owner tried to _____ the star player to join the team by offering him a large salary.

4. Looking to incite the players on the home team, the runner said something _____ about the first baseman's wife.

5. In an earlier era, it was common for people to refer to an attractive woman as being _____ .

6. The insurance adjuster was very _____ and serious about her work.

7. Stalkers are _____ with the celebrities they follow.

8. It is my personal _____ that Tibet should be free.

9. Sensual and captivating, her perfume was very _____ .

10. Initially, she couldn't figure out how to answer the question, but then she had a _____ and solved it right away.

11. She is _____ to cigarettes; she wants to smoke all the time.

12. Given the clues, the police _____ who was responsible for the robbery.

13. Lack of shelter is one of the many _____ of the homeless.

14. Movie villains are always hatching some _____ plot to take over the world.

15. He always gives in because he's _____ to trying to make others happy.

16. The United States is hoping more countries will _____ to rebuild Iraq.

17. The lab needed to _____ the water for pollutants.

18. The defense had suppressed some evidence, so the jury was not _____ of the full facts of the case.

19. The player was thrown out of the game because of the _____ foul he committed.

20. Eating chocolate is a _____ pleasure.

21. There has been a lot of _____ in the media about who will win the election.

22. Abandoning friends in the face of trouble is a _____ act.

23. He was fired for his _____ in the office scandal.

24. The Greek scholar Socrates is considered one of history's most _____ thinkers.

SYNONYM SENTENCES

In these sentences, use a form or tense of the words below to match their **bolded** synonyms, and write your choice in the space provided following each sentence.

Addiction	Conjecture	Obsession
Affliction	Conviction	Predisposition
Alluring	Crass	Profound
Assay	Craven	Revelation
Cognizant	Decoy	Sensual
Collaborate	Entice	Sinister
Comely	Flagrant	Stolid
Complicit	Irate	Surmise

WORD BANK

1. Saving yourself when others are in danger is **cowardly**. _____
2. The two companies will **cooperate** to make the project work.
3. The appraiser will **determine** the antique's value. _____
4. It is my **belief** that all people deserve proper health care. _____
5. He used his charm to **persuade** her to go out with him. _____
6. She is **prone** to getting seasick very easily. _____

7. Her perfume had an **appealing** scent. _____

8. Loud and obnoxious, he often makes **rude** remarks. _____

9. When she saw that she had received a parking ticket, she became **angry**. _____

10. Unable to control himself, he finally accepted that he was **dependent**. _____

11. Without sufficient information, we can only **guess** what the results will be. _____

12. The guard who opened the lock for the burglars was **involved** in the crime. _____

13. The celebrity's two-day marriage was a **blatant** attempt to gain publicity. _____

14. In her day, Jacqueline Kennedy was quite **attractive**. _____

15. She was **aware** of the implication of her actions. _____

16. During the spring, many people are **burdened** by allergies. _____

17. He isn't flashy at all; he's just a straightforward, **boring** kind of guy. _____

18. Silk is renowned for its supple, smooth, **pleasing** texture. _____

19. Electrical appliances have had a **significant** impact on the way we live. _____

20. By examining the rings of a tree stump, we can **deduce** how old the tree was when it was cut down. _____

21. Socks were a **compulsion** of his and he had hundreds of pairs in every color, pattern, and size. _____

22. The shocking **discovery** of criminal acts within the department caused a lot of disruption within the community. _____

23. In a bait-and-switch scam, an unscrupulous business will try to sell customers an inferior product by using a better product as a **lure**. _____

24. In video clips, Osama bin Laden reveals a **creepy** smile when he discusses the attack on the World Trade Center. _____

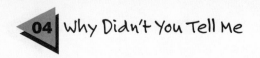
ᴛʜᴇ **ARTICLE**

Read the following article and then, for each question, select the one statements that best describes the authors' remarks.

Question 1

(a) Nina began working with Defined Mind shortly after coming to NYC.
(b) She works with the City of New York.
(c) Collaborating with Defined Mind made Nina soulful.
(d) None of the above

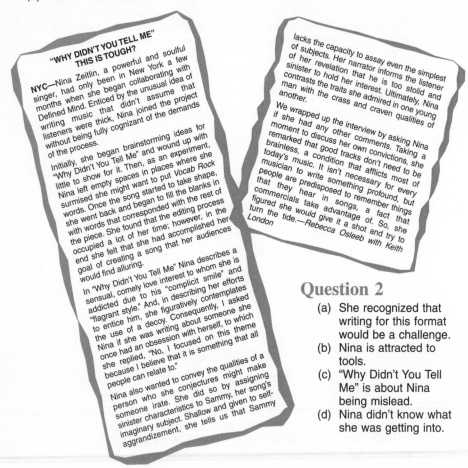

"WHY DIDN'T YOU TELL ME"
THIS IS TOUGH?

NYC—Nina Zeitlin, a powerful and soulful singer, had only been in New York a few months when she began collaborating with Defined Mind. Enticed by the unusual idea of writing music that didn't assume that listeners were thick, Nina joined the project without being fully cognizant of the demands of the process.

Initially, she began brainstorming ideas for "Why Didn't You Tell Me" and wound up with little to show for it. Then, as an experiment, Nina left empty spaces in places where she surmised she might want to put Vocab Rock words. Once the song started to take shape, she went back and began to fill the blanks in with words that corresponded with the rest of the piece. She found that the editing process occupied a lot of her time; however, in the end she felt that she had accomplished her goal of creating a song that her audiences would find alluring.

In "Why Didn't You Tell Me" Nina describes a sensual, comely love interest to whom she is addicted due to his "complicit smile" and "flagrant style." And, in describing her efforts to entice him, she figuratively contemplates the use of a decoy. Consequently, I asked Nina if she was writing about someone she once had an obsession with herself, to which she replied, "No, I focused on this theme because I believe that it is something that all people can relate to."

Nina also wanted to convey the qualities of a person who she conjectures might make someone irate. She did so by assigning sinister characteristics to Sammy, her song's imaginary subject. Shallow and given to self-aggrandizement, she tells us that Sammy

lacks the capacity to assay even the simplest of subjects. Her narrator informs the listener of her revelation that he is too stolid and sinister to hold her interest. Ultimately, Nina contrasts the traits she admired in one young man with the crass and craven qualities of another.

We wrapped up the interview by asking Nina if she had any other comments. Taking a moment to discuss her own convictions, she remarked that good tracks don't need to be brainless, a condition that afflicts most of today's music. It isn't necessary for every musician to write something profound, but people are predisposed to remember things that they hear in songs, a fact that commercials take advantage of. So, she figured she would give it a shot and try to turn the tide.—Rebecca Osleeb with Keith London

Question 2

(a) She recognized that writing for this format would be a challenge.
(b) Nina is attracted to tools.
(c) "Why Didn't You Tell Me" is about Nina being mislead.
(d) Nina didn't know what she was getting into.

Question 3
- (a) Nina was accustomed to writing for brains.
- (b) She was interested in writing in a new idiom.
- (c) She complained that this would be too difficult.
- (d) Nina is cognizant of difficult procedures.

Question 4
- (a) She had a brainstorm.
- (b) Nina likes to hunt ducks using decoys.
- (c) She was inspired to write the song and complete it afterward.
- (d) None of the above

Question 5
- (a) Nina likes to wear masks to hide her feelings.
- (b) To gain her love interest's attention, she contemplates the use of a lure.
- (c) She is addicted to dentistry and outrageous styles.
- (d) Nina contemplates writing a poem to her crush to tell him how she feels.

Question 6
- (a) Nina appreciates her crush's knowing, sly smile and confident demeanor.
- (b) She becomes angry because his smile and style is much nicer than hers.
- (c) She admires Sammy for his good looks and style but doesn't like him.
- (d) Nina is sensual and comely.

Question 7
- (a) The editing process was fast and efficient.
- (b) She corresponded with others who write for Defined Mind.
- (c) Nina wrote the song by allotting her time.
- (d) Editing the song took a great deal of time.

Question 8
- (a) Nina believes that she wrote a great song.
- (b) She wants to attract someone utilizing music.
- (c) Her audiences are attracted to her.
- (d) She created a song that is difficult to find.

Question 9
- (a) In "Why Didn't You Tell Me" Nina says that she's addicted to love.
- (b) Her love interest doesn't smile and has no style.
- (c) Nina wrote about a comely, outgoing young man.
- (d) She is a sensual person with an attractive appearance.

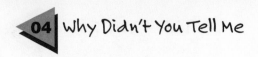

Question 10

(a) Sammy is an example of a wonderful man.
(b) Sammy exists as a subject in this song to convey unattractive qualities.
(c) Nina would like to date Sammy.
(d) Sammy can hold a conversation about any subject.

Question 11

(a) She wants to write commercials.
(b) She wants to take advantage of commercials.
(c) Nina is afflicted by brainless music.
(d) Nina feels it is easier to remember information from songs.

"I would love to learn to play something so I don't have to rely on someone to **collaborate** with."
—*Gwen Stefani*

Listening Exercise

Listen to "Go!" all the way through at least once. Then listen to the song again, and graffiti up the wall with any new or unfamiliar words that you hear. Don't worry if you don't fill up the whole wall . . . although we can hardly fathom why you couldn't!

GO! | Keith Middleton & Rodney Willie | Lyrics by Rodney Willie | Music Written & Performed by Keith Middleton | Vocals: Rodney Willie | Additional Vocals: Keith Middleton | Produced by Keith Middleton | Technical Producer: Craig Chang

LYRICS

| Get on your mark (Mark!) | Ready, set, Go! | Get on your mark (Mark!) | Ready, set, Go! | Get on your mark (Mark!) | Ready, set, Go! | I ain't rhymin' too fast | Y'all just listen too slow (2x) | Go! | **ANNIHILATE** 'em with the next flow | **MOMENTOUS** are my sentences | **SIGNIFICANT** for rocking shows | I'm dropping those (What?! What?!) **LABYRINTHINE** rhyme patterns | **INTRICATE PARADIGMS** that your mind can't **FATHOM** | My designs leave 'em **PERPLEXED** and scratching their temples | **CONTEXT** is **COMPLEX**, **ANTITHESIS** of simple | And if you **DECIPHER** my words, I give you **CREDIT** | Very few can see it clearly, so that makes you **ESOTERIC** | That **MERITS** you honor | to **PROCURE** an award | The highest of **ACCOLADES** while an audience applauds | My **EXPERTISE** to bring me everything that money can afford | Rest **ASSURED**, warlord with a pen for my sword | See my mind's my Nine, my pen is my Mack Ten | Use 'em both when up close and ready for action | You get blinded by the diamonds shining from light **REFRACTION** | It's all **INCONSEQUENTIAL**, just a minor **DISTRACTION** | Get on your mark (Mark!) | Ready, set, Go! | Get on your mark (Mark!) | Ready, set, Go! | Get on your mark (Mark!) | Ready, set, Go! | I ain't rhymin' too fast | Y'all just listen too slow (2x) | I am the **EPITOME** of everything MCs wanna be | **REVERE** me | More important tell people to act **ACCORDINGLY** | Recording the audio **FREQUENCY FREQUENTLY** leaves | **LESSER** MCs **PUSILLANIMOUS** acting cowardly | My poetic spirit **BORDERS** on the **PUGILISTIC** | You need a mouthpiece and a helmet to be safe when you hear it | So don't get too close (Nooo!!) | This verbal **VIRTUOSO** | Will leave you in **VERTIGO** | When my voice puts you in choke holds | Taped up with bandages seeking **PUNITIVE** damages | I got the point of **VANTAGE** on rappers, labels, and managers | These cats is **AMATEURS**, **NEOPHYTES** against a professional | So don't feel too bad when you see that it's me that just **BESTED** you | Get on your mark (Mark!) | Ready, set, Go! | Get on

your mark (Mark!) | Ready, set, Go! | Get on your mark (Mark!) | Ready, set, Go! | I ain't rhymin' too fast | Y'all just listen too slow (2x) | On your mark (On your mark) | If you're ready (Get ready) | Get set (Get set) | Here we go! (Here we go!) | Let's Go! | Get on your mark (Mark!) | Ready, set, Go! | Get on your mark (Mark!) | Ready, set, Go! | Get on your mark (Mark!) | Ready, set, Go! | I ain't rhymin' too fast | Y'all just listen too slow (2x) | (Ad lib)

dic•tion•ar•y

Accolade (n)—praise, award; great compliment. Antonym: insult (n).
Her film started receiving accolades shortly after it premiered, and it ultimately went on to win her an Oscar.
Accordingly (adv)—1. suitably.
Wanting to make a good impression on her interview, she dressed accordingly.
Accordingly (adv)—2. consequently; as a result of.
His neighbor threatened to sue him, and accordingly, he retained a lawyer.
Amateur (n)—layperson; one who participates in an activity for recreation. Antonym: professional (n).
It was his first time surfing and he looked like an amateur.
Annihilate (v)—destroy, kill; idiomatically used to describe superiority in competition.
Our team annihilated the visitors in this past weekend's game.
Antithesis (n)—opposite, converse.
New York City is the antithesis of a small town.
Assure (v)—guarantee, promise.
The salesman assured me that I was getting a great deal.
Bested (v)—beaten, surpassed; to be defeated or outclassed.
Their team had more practice than ours, and consequently, they bested us.
Border (v)—1. to be on the verge of or to approximate something.
His infatuation with grisly video games borders on mental illness.

Border (v)—2. to be physically adjacent to something.
Manhattan and Queens both border the East River.
Border (n)—3. boundary.
The United States and Canada share a border.
Complex (adj)—intricate, difficult. Antonym: simple (adj).
Between little black boxes and onboard diagnostic systems, today's cars are far too complex for people to repair on their own.
Context (n)—circumstances; details surrounding a subject.
On the news his quote seemed harsh; his remark was actually benign, but it had been taken out of context.
Credit (n)—recognition, acknowledgment. Antonym: blame (n).
I wouldn't have been able to write the book without her, so I wanted to give her due credit.
Decipher (v)—decode, grasp; to figure out.
I couldn't decipher her handwriting and was therefore unable to respond to her note.
Distraction (n)—disturbance, diversion, interruption. Antonym: focus (n).
Listening to music while I work is a distraction.
Epitome (n)—essence, height, archetype, embodiment; perfect example.
Jacqueline Kennedy was the epitome of style and grace in the days of Camelot.
Esoteric (adj)—perplexing, arcane. Antonym: straightforward (adj).
Their conversation was too esoteric and I couldn't understand anything they were talking about.
Expertise (n)—knowledge, skill, proficiency.
Programming computers requires expertise.
Fathom (v)—comprehend, understand, grasp.
I can't fathom why he thought it would be okay to stay out until sunrise on the night before a college interview.
Frequency (n)—1. the bandwidth of broadcast radio or television signals.
She wanted to listen to her favorite radio station during our road trip, but we couldn't get that frequency.
Frequency (n)—2. the pitch or tone of sound waves.
The frequency of the whistle can only be heard by dogs.
Frequency (n)—3. rate of occurrence or recurrence.
Accidents occur at that intersection with alarming frequency.
Frequently (adv)—regularly, repeatedly, habitually.
He's very absent-minded and he frequently loses his keys.

Inconsequential (adj)—unimportant, minor, trivial. Antonym: important (adj).
Their remarks were completely inconsequential and had no bearing on her decision.

Intricate (adj)—complex, complicated. Antonym: simple (adj).
Computers are too intricate for most people to repair on their own.

Labyrinthine (adj)—circuitous, convoluted. Antonym: direct (adj).
The narrow, winding streets of Venice are a labyrinthine maze that seems to have been thrown together over the centuries.

Lesser (adj)—smaller; less significant. Antonym: greater (adj).
I don't like either of the candidates very much and feel that I'll need to choose between the lesser of two evils.

Merits (v)—1. to warrant or deserve.
Her bravery merits the highest honor.

Merits (n)—2. benefits, pros. Antonym: disadvantages (n).
She was hired based upon her merits.

Momentous (adj)—important, considerable, historic. Antonym: inconsequential (adj).
The Apollo 11 moon landing was a momentous accomplishment for mankind.

Neophyte (n)—beginner, novice. Antonym: veteran (n).
Everyone starts as a neophyte and builds expertise with practice.

Paradigm (n)—example, model, standard.
Julia Child established the paradigm for today's cooking programs.

Perplex (v)—confuse, confound, befuddle. Antonym: clarify (v).
We were perplexed by the intricate directions.

Procure (v)—obtain, acquire. Antonym: divest (v).
She couldn't repair it until she had procured the correct tool.

Pugilistic (adj)—quarrelsome, belligerent; related to boxing. Antonym: conciliatory (adj).
Embroiled in a heated argument, they each adopted a pugilistic stance as they tried to shout down one another.

Punitive (adj)—corrective, retaliatory; inflicting punishment.
Since the company refused to make amends for their mistake, she was compelled to take punitive action.

Pusillanimous (adj)—cowardly, craven, timid. Antonym: courageous (adj).
Pusillanimous in the extreme, the prince sent others off to wage his battles.

Refraction (n)—the change in direction of light or sound wave as it passes from one material into another.
Although it may look as though your spoon is bending when you place it in a glass of water, it is actually an illusion created by refraction.

Revere (v)—admire, worship. Antonym: revile (v).
Michael Jordan is revered for his skills on the basketball court.

Significant (adj)—meaningful, consequential. Antonym: insignificant (adj).
The school made significant changes to its curriculum to accommodate the new regulations.

Vantage (n)—1. advantage. Antonym: disadvantage (n).
Positioned above the valley, our forces had the vantage against the invading army.

Vantage (n)—2. perspective.
Positioned above the valley, our forces had an excellent vantage point to observe the invading army's troop movements.

Vertigo (n)—dizziness; confused state of mind.
He had an unbearable fear of heights and was overcome by vertigo whenever he entered a tall building.

Virtuoso (n)—1. genius, prodigy; someone with masterful skill in the arts.
She's been playing the piano since she was a toddler, and now she's a virtuoso who headlines performances around the world.

Virtuoso (adj)—2. exhibiting the ability or technique of a genius or prodigy.
Windows® is only one of Bill Gates's virtuoso creations.

SYNONYM MATCHI♫G

Match the following words with their synonyms. Note the letter of the matching synonym in the space adjacent to the word.

_____ Accolades

_____ Accordingly

_____ Amateur

_____ Annihilate

_____ Antithesis

_____ Assure

_____ Bested

_____ Borders

_____ Complex

_____ Context

_____ Credit

_____ Decipher

_____ Distraction

_____ Epitome

_____ Esoteric

_____ Expertise

_____ Fathom

_____ Frequency

_____ Frequently

_____ Inconsequential

_____ Intricate

_____ Labyrinthine

_____ Lesser

_____ Merits

_____ Momentous

_____ Neophyte

_____ Paradigm

_____ Perplex

_____ Procure

_____ Pugilistic

_____ Punitive

_____ Pusillanimous

_____ Refraction

_____ Revere

_____ Significant

_____ Vantage

_____ Vertigo

_____ Virtuoso

(a) decode
(b) on the verge of
(c) proficiency
(d) surpassed
(e) regularly
(f) comprehend
(g) dizziness
(h) disturbance
(i) belligerent
(j) novice
(k) trivial
(l) praise
(m) consequently
(n) rate of occurrence
(o) intricate
(p) layperson
(q) guarantee
(r) essence
(s) opposite
(t) recognition
(u) timid
(v) admire
(w) advantage
(x) change in direction
(y) circumstances
(z) historic
(a1) circuitous
(a2) meaningful
(a3) prodigy
(a4) arcane
(a5) to deserve
(a6) complicated
(a7) retaliatory
(a8) example
(a9) smaller
(b1) confuse
(b2) destroy
(b3) acquire

sentencecompl@tion

Using a form or tense of the words below, find the one to best complete each of the following sentences.

WORD BANK

Accolades	Credit	Intricate	Pugilistic
Accordingly	Decipher	Labyrinthine	Punitive
Amateur	Distraction	Lesser	Pusillanimous
Annihilate	Epitome	Merits	Refraction
Antithesis	Esoteric	Momentous	Revere
Assure	Expertise	Neophyte	Significant
Bested	Fathom	Paradigm	Vantage
Borders	Frequency	Perplex	Vertigo
Complex	Frequently	Procure	Virtuoso
Context			

1. We have an easy time talking to each other because we're on the same _____ .

2. Many academic institutions are working to improve the state of education and are seeking a new _____ .

3. He played masterfully and we were treated to a _____ performance.

4. Complex is the _____ of simple.

5. The study's outcome is encouraging and _____ further study.

6. The route we took was _____ , and there isn't any way we would be able to get back without better directions.

7. It was pretty pathetic that they were _____ by one of the worst teams in the league.

8. She's worked in the discipline for many years and has accumulated significant _____ on that particular subject.

9. The roller coaster was too much for him and he was overcome by _____ .

10. It looked intimidating, but we _____ him that it was safe.

11. _____ is the antithesis of simple.

12. Our team _____ the competition and we finished the season undefeated.

13. The chemistry professor instructed us to behave _____ in the lab because, otherwise, we might blow ourselves to bits.

14. We couldn't _____ why he went to school wearing a pink tutu.

15. During their discussion, she convinced him to see the issue from her _____ point.

16. Like everyone else, I started out as a _____ , but my expertise grew with training and experience.

17. He gave up his _____ ranking and went pro this season.

18. When I brought up the topic, she became _____ , but her tone softened as she came to understand my perspective.

19. I find flashing online ads very _____ ; they make it difficult to read a site's content.

20. She works at a think tank in Washington, D.C., and spends her time pondering "buy-side economics" and other _____ subjects.

21. Even after hours of interrogation, he wouldn't _____ the secret code for his captors.

22. I'll readily acknowledge that it was originally her idea; I have to give _____ where it's due.

23. It is always gratifying to receive _____ and the respect of your peers.

24. His recent unusual behavior _____ on insanity.

25. The new data we received was _____ and did not affect our original findings.

26. Since she didn't have any good options, she was forced to choose between the _____ of two evils.

27. He was _____ by the toy's complicated assembly instructions.

28. The Dali Lama is _____ for his wisdom and spiritual insight.

29. Always ready to come through in the clutch, she _____ grace under pressure.

30. Never _____ , he fought for what was right.

31. A diamond sparkles because light is _____ as it shines through its facets.

32. We need to _____ some additional equipment before we embark on our camping trip.

33. To best understand historical events, it is important that we view them in _____ .

34. I'm _____ preoccupied and forgetful; if my head weren't attached to my shoulders, I would have already lost it somewhere.

35. Chastising the defendant, the judge awarded the plaintiff $100 million in _____ damages.

36. The findings of the study were _____ and caused us to reconsider our position on the issue.

37. Christening the new ship, the captain remarked, "I would like to say a few words in honor of this _____ occasion."

38. He was perplexed by the toy's _____ assembly instructions.

SYNONYM SENTENCES

In these sentences, use a form or tense of the words below to match their **bolded** synonyms, and write your choice in the space provided following each sentence.

Accolades	Credit	Intricate	Pugilistic
Accordingly	Decipher	Labyrinthine	Punitive
Amateur	Distraction	Lesser	Pusillanimous
Annihilate	Epitome	Merits	Refraction
Antithesis	Esoteric	Momentous	Revere
Assure	Expertise	Neophyte	Significant
Bested	Fathom	Paradigm	Vantage
Borders	Frequency	Perplex	Vertigo
Complex	Frequently	Procure	Virtuoso
Context			

WORD BANK

1. Her reasoning was **convoluted,** and I still cannot fathom how she arrived at her conclusions. _____

2. Even though the theater company is **recreational**, their production of *Death of a Salesman* was excellent. _____

3. Outgoing and friendly, he is the **opposite** of his curmudgeonly father. _____

4. She's in great shape because she exercises **regularly**. _____

5. The defenders **destroyed** the invading forces as they fought to enter the city. _____

6. His partner created a **diversion** while he absconded with the paintings. _____

7. Her physician was concerned about her condition; **consequently**, he conducted a battery of tests to establish a diagnosis. _____

8. He said that although he authored the piece, she deserves much of the **recognition** for their accomplishment. _____

9. He was overcome by **dizziness** on the Empire State Building's observation deck. _____

10. It takes years to learn to read and write in Chinese because the language's characters are so **intricate**. _____

11. Hearing barking on a CD that I was playing, my dog stared at the speaker, **confused** as to why she couldn't find the other dogs. _____

12. She couldn't possibly **comprehend** that the dogs' barks were recorded and overdubbed into the song. _____

13. The engineers selected the design based upon its **benefits**. _____

14. The design was well regarded and received a variety of **compliments**. _____

15. She **beat** me in three games out of four. _____

16. I **promised** him we would arrive to the airport in time to make his flight. _____

17. In college you have the opportunity to explore **arcane** subject matter that you wouldn't normally encounter outside of an academic setting. _____

18. She was **admired** for her longstanding role as the community's spiritual leader and its most determined advocate. _____

19. Underhanded and **craven**, he ratted out his cronies to the feds to save his own skin. _____

20. He considers lobbying to be a **less significant** influence on public policy than it is popularly thought to be. _____

21. The completion of the Brooklyn Bridge was a **historic** event that marked the dawn of a new age in engineering. _____

22. She recently earned another belt in karate, but she's still a **novice** and has a lot of work to do to build her expertise. _____

23. She gave a **masterful** performance at Carnegie Hall and received a standing ovation. _____

24. The issue is far more **complicated** than I had first thought, and I'll need to give it further consideration before I make a decision. _____

25. While visiting Rome, I asked our guide to translate a shopkeeper's comments because I couldn't **grasp** what he was trying to say. _____

26. I wouldn't call his contributions trivial, but they weren't very **meaningful** either. _____

27. I'm not sure how I will respond to her comments; I imagine it will depend on the **circumstances**. _____

28. My kid brother's new remote-control truck didn't work because the remote-control unit was on a different **bandwidth**. _____

29. While the article does bring some new information to light, much of it **verges** on fiction. _____

30. They couldn't hire her because she did not possess the necessary **skill set**. _____

31. When she asked him to turn off his cell phone during the performance, he became **belligerent**. _____

32. She acquiesced to his requests because they were ultimately to her **advantage**. _____

33. The rover sustained a jolt when it landed, but any damage was **minimal**. _____

34. Since our neighbors weren't willing to repair the damage they caused, our attorney recommended that we take **corrective** measures. _____

35. In order to execute the plan in its current form, it will be necessary for us to **acquire** additional resources. _____

36. Both light and sound waves experience **a change in direction** as they pass through different materials. _____

37. General George S. Patton was the **embodiment** of the war-hardened military man. _____

38. In 1954 Steve Allen created the **model** for the modern talk show. _____

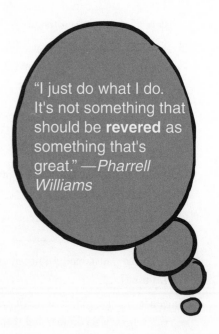

"I just do what I do. It's not something that should be **revered** as something that's great." —*Pharrell Williams*

THE ARTICLE

Read the following article and then, for each question, select the one statement that best describes the authors' remarks.

RODNEY WILLIE IS READY TO "GO!"

NYC—Rodney Willie, who's known in most contexts as "RW" but credited on *Vocab Rock* by his real name, is a lyrical virtuoso who can easily best the most pugilistic MC. Keith Middleton, his musical alter ego and the epitome of talent and professionalism, is assuredly the antithesis of an amateur and merits his own praise, but upon fathoming the expertise revealed in "Go!" I must give Rodney his due accolades.

As far as I can decipher, his key vantage is that his significant intellect borders on genius. Refracted through his muse, his labyrinthine rhymes put lesser recording artists to shame. His deft use of words annihilates the stereotypes of a hardened street rapper, and he procures an esoteric paradigm unrivaled by any that I have encountered before. Pusillanimous neophytes may be perplexed by the intricacy of his verse, but accordingly, those in the know revere him for the momentous accomplishment that they represent. Any remarks to the contrary are simply punitive.

Complex in the extreme, Rodney's raps frequently bring me to the verge of vertigo when trying to keep up with him in the studio. However, we're always on the same frequency when it comes to the qualities that we're looking to instill in the tracks, and any distractions ultimately prove to be inconsequential.—Keith London and Rebecca Osleeb

Question 1

(a) RW is belligerent, and the name on his *Vocab Rock* credit card is "Rodney Willie."

(b) The table of contents credits him as "RW" but *Vocab Rock* calls him "Rodney Willie."

(c) Most people call Rodney "RW," but on *Vocab Rock* he is credited as "Rodney Willie."

(d) Rodney calls himself "RW," but he asked our staff to address him as "Mr. Willie."

Question 2

(a) The author believes that Rodney is a verbal prodigy and a great boxer.

(b) The author regards Rodney as a verbal genius who can surpass even the toughest competitor.

(c) Rodney plays the lyric beautifully and his best pet pug is named "MC."

(d) Rodney's performance is pure genius and has been called "The Boxing MC."

Question 3

(a) Keith Middleton, who writes the music, is an outstanding professional who deserves his own accolades.

(b) Keith's converse essence deserves its own guarantees.

(c) Keith, who writes the music to Rodney's lyrics, says that he is a professional.

(d) Keith Middleton is the epitome of alter egos, and the author guarantees that he is an amateur.

Question 4

(a) Rodney asked the author to give him the award that he was withholding.

(b) The author couldn't fathom how RW could reveal his expertise to win an award.

(c) "Go!" compelled the author to honor Rodney with an award for proficiency.

(d) "Go!" prompted the author to take inventory of Rodney's skill and to compliment him.

Question 5

(a) The author is looking to decode Rodney's primary advantage.

(b) The author believes that Rodney's primary advantage is his considerable intellect.

(c) The author is having trouble figuring out how Rodney's point of view influences his work.

(d) The author has been working to determine Rodney's intellectual boundaries.

Question 6

(a) Rodney enjoys embarrassing other performers by using a muse to bend the light in his maze.

(b) Rodney's muse bends sound waves, which results in convoluted rhymes.

(c) Rodney's towering verses are the product of great inspiration and make other recording artists look inferior.

(d) Rodney likes to shame other recording artists via his labyrinthine rhymes.

Question 7

(a) The author feels that Rodney's work dispels the notion that artists who rap are incapable of authoring intellectually challenging material.

(b) Rodney destroys stereotypes by acquiring arcane models.

(c) Rodney is a hardened street rapper who said something arcane to the author.

(d) All of the above

Question 8

(a) Cowardly beginners are confused by Rodney, but those who understand his work worship him.

(b) Timid novices may be befuddled by the complexity of Rodney's work, but appropriately, those who are knowledgeable admire its significance.

(c) Rodney is worshiped and admired by those in-the-know, whereas timid beginners are befuddled by the complexity of his lyrics.

(d) None of the above

Question 9

(a) Anyone who disagrees with the author will be sued for punitive damages.
(b) Anyone who makes remarks that conflict with the author's will be punished.
(c) Anyone who disagrees with the author needs to be corrected.
(d) Those who do not believe that Rodney's work is brilliant are just jealous.

Question 10

(a) Rodney enjoys extreme sports that regularly make people dizzy.
(b) Rodney regularly makes his colleagues dizzy in the studio.
(c) The intricacy of Rodney's lyrics regularly makes the author dizzy.
(d) The complexity of Rodney's extremities gives the author vertigo.

Question 11

(a) The author would like Rodney to turn off the radio because it interrupts him.
(b) Despite the quality of the equipment he is using, Rodney cannot find the radio station he and the author both enjoy.
(c) Rodney and the author work together well, and disruptions that might otherwise interfere with their progress prove to be insignificant.
(d) All of the above

Acquiesce Amorous Aroma Awkward Consummate
Conversely Deleterious Delirium Ecstasy Enamored Futile
Incantation Inevitably Infatuation Inimitable Interminable
Intuit Laborious Prosimity Reticence Senescent Shroud
Situation Synchronously Tortuous Tranquility Acquiesce
Amorous Aroma Awkward Consummate Conversely
Deleterious Delirium Ecstasy Enamored Futile Incantation
Inevitably Infatuation Inimitable Interminable Intuit Laborious
Prosimity Reticence Senescent Shroud Situation
Synchronously Tortuous Tranquility Acquiesce Amorous
Aroma Awkward Consummate Conversely Deleterious
Delirium Ecstasy Enamored Futile Incantation Inevitably
Infatuation Inimitable Interminable Intuit Laborious Prosimity
Reticence Senescent Shroud Situation Synchronously
Tortuous Tranquility Acquiesce Amorous Aroma Awkward
Consummate Conversely Deleterious Delirium Ecstasy
Enamored Futile Incantation Inevitably Infatuation Inimitable
Interminable Intuit Laborious Prosimity Reticence Senescent
Shroud Situation Synchronously Tortuous Tranquility
Acquiesce Amorous Aroma Awkward Consummate
Conversely Deleterious Delirium Ecstasy Enamored Futile
Incantation Inevitably Infatuation Inimitable Interminable
Intuit Laborious Prosimity Reticence Senescent Shroud
Situation Synchronously Tortuous Tranquility Acquiesce
Amorous Aroma Awkward Consummate Conversely
Deleterious Delirium Ecstasy Enamored Futile Incantation
Inevitably Infatuation Inimitable Interminable Intuit Laborious Prosimity
Reticence Senescent Shroud Situation Synchronously
Tortuous Tranquility Acquiesce Amorous Aroma Awkward
Consummate Conversely Deleterious Delirium Ecstasy
Enamored Futile Incantation Inevitably Infatuation Inimitable

Troy Jackson of F.A.M.E. Ent.

SUPERGIRL

Listening Exercise

Listen to "SuperGirl" all the way through at least once. Then listen to the song again, and graffiti up the wall with any new or unfamiliar words that you hear. Don't worry if you don't fill up the whole wall . . . but do resolve to give it your best shot!

SUPERGIRL | Adrienne Hecker & Lyle Beers | Lyrics by Adrienne Hecker | Music Written & Performed by Lyle Beers | Vocals: Adrienne Hecker | Produced by Mike Pandolfo & Lyle Beers

LYRICS

| With **CANDOR** we say **PITHY** things | We must confess about our **MINIMAL RESOLVE** | Now that the **TOXIN'S SEEPED** into our veins | Can't **FATHOM** simple things | This thing's so **INFINITE** | I come away from the fire a **PHOENIX** | Journeying towards the big hot sun | I'm your SuperGirl, **TRAVERSING** the **COSMOS** | In a super world, uniting the **FACTIONS** | SuperGirl, my **DECLARATION** : | Turn in your guns and **MANIFEST** love | Don't **SLANDER**, we've lost no love | Can't **SQUANDER** precious time | On things that don't **LOOM** large | It's so **CRUCIAL** to just live **GRACIOUSLY** | Let us **BESTOW** our gifts | And watch the hate **DISSOLVE** | I've come away from the **MIRE** a **GENIUS** | Returning now like a **BENEDICTION** | I'm your SuperGirl, **TRAVERSING** the **COSMOS** | In a super world, uniting the **FACTIONS** | SuperGirl, my **DECLARATION** : | Turn in your guns and **MANIFEST** love | Our **UNDERLYING** spark | Could **DISPEL** all of the darkness | With **AWESOME** pride | We'll gently glide through the atmosphere | With **AWESOME** pride | We'll gently glide through the atmosphere | **QUIXOTIC** behavior will yet be the savior | Of humanity when it comes undone | I'm your SuperGirl, **TRAVERSING** the **COSMOS** | In a super world, uniting the **FACTIONS** | SuperGirl, my **DECLARATION** : | Turn in your guns and **MANIFEST** love | I'm your SuperGirl, **TRAVERSING** the **COSMOS** | In a super world, uniting the **FACTIONS** | SuperGirl, my **DECLARATION** : | Turn in your guns and **MANIFEST** love | I'm your SuperGirl

dic•tion•ar•y

Awesome (adj)—great, awe-inspiring, amazing. Antonym: uninspiring (adj).
The Grand Canyon is an awesome sight.

Benediction (n)—blessing, approval; a prayer asking for help or protection. Antonym: curse (n).
The priest ended the service by reciting a benediction.

Bestow (v)—give, confer, grant. Antonym: rescind (v).
He bestowed his blessing upon his daughter's engagement.

Candor (n)—honesty, frankness, openness.
Looking for constructive criticism, I appreciated his candor.

Cosmos (n)—outer space; the universe.
The astronomer used a telescope to gaze out into the cosmos.

Crucial (adj)—essential; extremely important or necessary.
She said, "If you want to do well on the exam, it is crucial that you study."

Declaration (n)—statement, announcement; usually regarding a strong belief.
He was asked to submit a written declaration explaining what he witnessed during the accident.

Dispel (v)—dismiss, eliminate; cause to vanish.
To dispel the rumors of her illness, the councilwoman held a press conference at her gym.

Dissolve (v)—1. melt. Antonym: solidify (v).
The ice cube dissolved in his freshly brewed coffee.

Dissolve (v)—2. end, disband. Antonym: initiate (v).
The new military dictator dissolved the country's democratically elected legislature.

Faction (n)—group, clique, party; a group within a larger group.
Congress members representing competing interests frequently organize themselves into opposing factions.

Fathom (v)—comprehend, understand, grasp.
I can't fathom why he thought it would be okay to stay out until sunrise on the night before a college interview.

Genius (n)—brilliance; extraordinary intelligence or skill. Antonym: stupidity (n).
She's a genius and finishes her exams in record time.

Graciously (adv)—politely; behaving in a courteous manner.
Giving all of the credit to the team, she graciously accepted the award for MVP.

Infinite (adj)—never-ending, endless, uncountable. Antonym: finite (adj).
As far as we can tell, the cosmos are infinite.

Loom (v)—1. overhang, appear, project; come into view. Antonym: recede (v).
We came in early from boating yesterday because a storm was looming on the horizon.

Loom (v)—2. philosophically resonate; have relevance.
Even today, Elvis Presley looms large on the music scene.

Manifest (v)—1. show; become evident or visible. Antonym: dissipate (v).
Her illness first manifested itself as a high fever.

Manifest (adj)—2. obvious, apparent. Antonym: subtle (adj).
He didn't know what transgression he committed to prompt her manifest hostility.

Minimal (adj)—the smallest amount or number allowed or possible. Antonym: maximum (adj).
The minimal number of credits needed to graduate is forty.

Mire (n)—1. a bog; gunk, marsh, swamp.
She lost her boot while walking through the mire.

Mire (n)—2. a difficult situation.
In the mire of their parents' divorce, she and her sister remained close and were able to use each other as sounding boards.

Phoenix (n)—1. a mythological bird that ignites itself into flames every 500 years and is born again from the ashes.
The phoenix rose again, reborn from its ashes.

Phoenix (n)—2. someone who resurrects or redeems themselves.
Despite having been bankrupt, he rose like a phoenix and made a great comeback.

Pithy (adj)—terse, concise; to the point. Antonym: rambling (adj).
Her attorney made a pithy remark in response to the plaintiff's comments.

Quixotic (adj)—idealistic but impractical.
The notion that all people will live in peace is nice but quixotic.

Resolve (v)—1. solve, decide.
Working together, we can resolve the problem.
Resolve (n)—2. conviction, determination, tenacity; dedication of purpose. Antonym: indifference (n).
Full of resolve, the stranded mountaineers made their treacherous descent to safety.
Seep (v)—leak, leach, bleed.
The paint seeped out of the can and wound up on everything in the bag.
Slander (v)—insult, malign, defame; make oral false and malicious statements. Antonym: praise (v).
Insisting he was faithful to his wife, he said the reporter slandered him by announcing that he was having an affair.
Squander (v)—waste.
My brother squandered his entire paycheck on a 30-pound stick of gum.
Toxin (n)—poison, pollutant, contaminant.
The industrial plant illegally released toxins that poisoned the local wildlife.
Traverse (v)—cross, travel, navigate; pass through.
Traveling by car, plane, and train, his mom is traversing the globe.
Underlying (adj)—fundamental; describes a principle upon which something is based or is influenced by; primary reason or influence.
Taxes are an underlying issue in the upcoming presidential race.

SYNONYM MATCHI♫G

Match the following words with their synonyms. Note the letter of the matching synonym in the space adjacent to the word.

_____ Awesome

_____ Benediction

_____ Bestow

_____ Candor

_____ Cosmos

_____ Crucial

_____ Declaration

_____ Dispel

_____ Dissolve

_____ Faction

_____ Fathom

_____ Genius

_____ Gracious

_____ Infinite

_____ Loom

_____ Manifest

_____ Minimal

_____ Mire

_____ Phoenix

_____ Pithy

_____ Quixotic

_____ Resolve

_____ Seep

_____ Slander

_____ Squander

_____ Toxin

_____ Traversing

_____ Underlying

(a)	endless
(b)	idealistic
(c)	show
(d)	marsh
(e)	conviction
(f)	waste
(g)	primary influence
(h)	leak
(i)	defame
(j)	give
(k)	smallest
(l)	traveling
(m)	awe-inspiring
(n)	concise
(o)	blessing
(p)	understand
(q)	openness
(r)	essential
(s)	redeemed
(t)	dismiss
(u)	disband
(v)	statement
(w)	outer space
(x)	poison
(y)	group
(z)	overhang
(a1)	extraordinary intelligence
(a2)	polite

sentencecompl@tion

Using a form or tense of the words below, find the one to best complete each of the following sentences.

WORD BANK

Awesome	Dispel	Loom	Resolve
Benediction	Dissolve	Manifest	Seep
Bestow	Factions	Minimal	Slander
Candor	Fathom	Mire	Squander
Cosmos	Genius	Phoenix	Toxin
Crucial	Graciously	Pithy	Traversing
Declaration	Infinite	Quixotic	Underlying

1. The many _____ in the air are said to be the cause for the increase in cases of asthma in children.

2. He sought their approval as though it were a _____ .

3. She tried to _____ what caused her mom's angry reaction.

4. Using the microwave to cook takes a _____ amount of effort.

5. After she was offered a satisfactory, but not perfect, job, her dad told her not to _____ a good opportunity.

6. Looking at the stars, the universe appears to go on into _____ .

7. The revolt for political reform originally _____ itself as a series of student protests.

8. They had everything ready for our visit to their summer house and were very _____ hosts.

9. To look at Earth while walking on the moon must be an _____ sight.

10. The stadium proposal was contested by two _____ , people who supported its construction and others who were against it.

11. After shuffling their lineup, the last-place team came back like a _____ and went on to win the championship.

12. I could see the tornado _____ on the horizon, so we left the house to look for a safe place.

13. It is _____ to believe that we can eliminate world hunger.

14. The two of them were _____ in a longstanding argument.

15. I wish they would just sit down, talk it out, and _____ it.

16. The winner voluntarily submitted herself to a physical to _____ any allegations that she was using anything to enhance her performance.

17. At the start of the initiation ceremony, the new inductees made a _____ of faith to the secret society.

18. Occasionally, I gaze at the night sky and stare into the _____ .

19. Oil _____ from the tank, contaminating the surrounding soil.

20. He was always respected for his _____ , even though sometimes he was too honest.

21. The complexity of Mozart's musical composition is evidence of his _____ .

22. Following the TV reporter's claim that she was a criminal, she sued him for _____ .

23. Place the pill on your tongue and let it _____ .

24. The Purple Heart is a medal _____ on soldiers for suffering injuries in combat.

25. She apologized for her _____ response to my naive question.

26. It is _____ that you follow the medication's directions.

27. Lewis and Clark are famous for _____ the Louisiana Territory.

28. She disagreed with him because she thought his _____ assumptions were wrong.

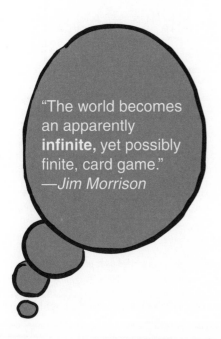

"The world becomes an apparently **infinite,** yet possibly finite, card game."
—*Jim Morrison*

SYNONYM SENTENCES

In these sentences, use a form or tense of the words below to match their **bolded** synonyms, and write your choice in the space provided following each sentence.

Awesome	Dispel	Loom	Resolve
Benediction	Dissolve	Manifest	Seep
Bestow	Factions	Minimal	Slander
Candor	Fathom	Mire	Squander
Cosmos	Genius	Phoenix	Toxin
Crucial	Graciously	Pithy	Traversing
Declaration	Infinite	Quixotic	Underlying

WORD BANK

1. I can't **understand** how she could deceive her best friend. _____

2. During high tide the harbor is filled with water, but while the tide is out it's a **bog**. _____

3. A few years ago he was down and out, but he worked hard to get his act together and came back like a **mythological bird**. _____

4. Although she was embarrassed to receive the attention of everyone at the event, she was humble and **politely** accepted the award. _____

5. Her aspirations were **idealistic**, but she persevered and succeeded. _____

6. The cosmos seems to be **endless** at night. _____

7. At the engagement party, the bride's father **gave** his blessings on the couple. _____

8. If you want to avoid sunburns, it is **essential** that you wear suntan lotion at the beach. _____

9. Architect Frank Gehry's buildings, some of which are constructed with wavy walls and titanium cladding, are regarded as works of pure **brilliance**. _____

10. The **smallest** amount of pay you can receive for this position is $6 an hour. _____

11. The **primary** reason he doesn't go to the movies is that he's afraid of the dark. _____

12. Reacting to the negative remarks that their paid spokesman made to the press, the company **ended** its relationship with him. _____

13. The sunrise broke over the horizon like a **blessing** on the new day. _____

14. Having set countless sales records, the Beatles' success still **resonates** throughout the music industry, even though they broke up more than thirty years ago. _____

15. Speaking about **poisons** that exist in nature, the horticulturist warned us that some wild mushrooms are deadly. _____

16. They **crossed** the mountain range. _____

17. Hoping he would forgive her, she **openly** told her boyfriend that she had dated another guy. _____

18. The new government was in a state of disarray because competing **groups** were fighting for power. _____

19. Looking to end the standoff, the union and corporate officers made a concerted effort to **solve** their differences. _____

20. The hotel room had an **amazing** view of the city skyline. _____

21. Genuinely concerned for his estranged sister's welfare, he showed up at the hospital to **eliminate** the idea that he didn't care. _____

22. Whenever I come into large amounts of money, I always seem to **waste** it. _____

23. At the movie premier, the star made a **terse** remark in response to an interviewer's question about her personal life. _____

24. The kids from another clique made **malicious** comments about my sister. _____

25. Bankrupt, addicted, and forsaken by her family, she **stated** that she would rebuild her life. _____

26. The planetarium show made me feel as though I were shooting through the **universe**. _____

27. I cut myself slicing a bagel, and the blood **leached** through the first bandage I put on. _____

28. She showed **obvious** relief at not having any more exams for the year. _____

THE ARTICLE

Read the following article and then, for each question, select the one statement that best describes the author's remarks.

HECKER AND BEERS LAUNCH "SUPERGIRL"

NYC—Just before a crucial recording session, we were enjoying some Vietnamese takeout with Adrienne Hecker and Lyle Beers at Native's loft studio, and they graciously agreed to a quick interview while we ate. In town to do the vocal tracks to "SuperGirl," they spoke candidly about their work together and the underlying philosophies that inspired the song.

Given the genius of their compositions, it surprised us to find that the pair has been writing together a minimal amount of time-- only one year. And it's awesome that they could manifest such a superlative declaration of resolve with so little prior collaboration. It dispelled our preconception that creative teams need a senescent partnership to produce great work.

Regarding "SuperGirl," its message looms large today, given how mired so many factions are in efforts to spread hatred's toxins. Lyle and Adrienne recognize the quixotic nature of hope for universal amity, but they said that it's hard for them to fathom how frequently people squander the peace that they do get.

Traversing the globe, this political party is slandering that political party while one leader is making pithy remarks to another leader. Adrienne and Lyle wonder when barriers are going to dissolve and permit settlement to rise like a phoenix. As we wrapped up our conversation and prepared to get to work, I thanked them for bestowing their benediction of reconciliation on us, and, as they said, "We can hope..."—Rebecca Osleeb

Question 1

(a) It was crucial that the authors and studio staff eat Vietnamese takeout.
(b) They were there to accomplish some important work.
(c) Native graciously offered the loft studio for a recording session.
(d) It was important that they ate before the recording session.

Question 2

(a) "SuperGirl" is a candid portrait of Lyle and Adrienne.
(b) The song's inspiring philosophical foundations are honest.
(c) They were in New York to record candid vocal tracks.
(d) The artists openly discussed the ideas behind "SuperGirl."

Question 3

  (a) The artists' compositions possess high I.Q.s.
  (b) Adrienne and Lyle are geniuses.
  (c) Lyle and Adrienne's music is brilliantly written.
  (d) The authors were surprised by the artists' intellects.

Question 4

  (a) The artists have been working together for only a short time.
  (b) Adrienne and Lyle have been a couple for only a short time.
  (c) The authors were surprised that they write together only minimally.
  (d) Their genius is illustrated by the minimal amount of time they need to write.

Question 5

  (a) The artists resolved to manifest a declaration.
  (b) The artists create great music despite working together only a short time.
  (c) The authors enjoy collaborating with superlatives.
  (d) With little prior collaboration, the artists and authors declared their resolve.

Question 6

  (a) "SuperGirl" echoes the *Declaration of Independence*.
  (b) "SuperGirl" manifests itself as a superlative.
  (c) "SuperGirl" is a statement regarding manifest destiny.
  (d) "SuperGirl" is a great statement of determination.

Question 7

  (a) The authors can't spell words related to creative concepts and unusual odors.
  (b) They produce great work because they know how partners should smell.
  (c) Originally, the authors thought only older partnerships could create great work.
  (d) Creative teams need a good sense of smell in order to produce great work.

Question 8

  (a) The song's theme revolves around factions caught in a sizable pile of muck.
  (b) The message of "SuperGirl" is fitting, given today's harsh sociopolitical climate.
  (c) "SuperGirl" is a song about a giant, weaving in a swamp.
  (d) The message in "SuperGirl" is fitting, given many groups' efforts to use poison.

Question 9

  (a) Adrienne and Lyle understand that hope for world peace is idealistic.
  (b) The artists recognize that natural events resemble the universe's version of *The Amityville Horror*.
  (c) Lyle and Adrienne know how to recognize Don Quixote.
  (d) The artists hope that universal amity is recognized for being quixotically natural.

Question 10

(a) They said that it is hard to work fathoms below the surface of the ocean because the fish interrupt their studio sessions.
(b) Lyle and Adrienne feel that people waste their opportunities for quiet and solitude.
(c) Adrienne and Lyle cannot fathom our frequent squandering.
(d) The artists can't understand why people choose to treat each other so poorly.

Question 11

(a) The artists slander political parties and make terse remarks to world leaders.
(b) Adrienne and Lyle belong to a political party that crosses the globe.
(c) Political parties and world leaders say unflattering things about one another.
(d) They make an observation regarding the excellent state of international relations.

Question 12

(a) The artists contemplate a time when people will cooperate and allow peace to flourish.
(b) Adrienne and Lyle are trying to figure out where they can find superpowers that will dissolve barriers.
(c) They want to acquire a mythical bird that can resurrect itself.
(d) None of the above

Question 13

(a) Lyle and Adrienne are ordained clergy and can grant blessings.
(b) The authors appreciated Adrienne and Lyle's wishes for world peace.
(c) At the end of their conversation, the artists bestowed a blessing upon the authors.
(d) At the end of their conversation, the authors thanked the artists for their blessings.

Acquiesce Amorous Aroma Awkward Consummate Conversely Deleterious Delirium Ecstasy Enamored Futile Incantation Inevitably Infatuation Inimitable Interminable Intuit Laborious Prosimity Reticence Senescent Shroud Situation Synchronously Tortuous Tranquility Acquiesce Amorous Aroma Awkward Consummate Conversely Deleterious Delirium Ecstasy Enamored Futile Incantation Inevitably Infatuation Inimitable Interminable Intuit Laborious Prosimity Reticence Senescent Shroud Situation Synchronously Tortuous Tranquility Acquiesce Aroma Awkward Consummate Conversely Deleterious Delirium Ecstasy Enamored Futile Inevitably Infatuation Inimitable Interminable Prosimity Reticence Senescent Shroud Situation Reticence Senescent Shroud Synchronously Tortuous Tranquility Awkward Consummate Ecstasy Enamored Inimitable Interminable Senescent Shroud Tranquility Acquiesce Consummate Conversely Enamored Futile Incantation Interminable Intuit Laborious Prosimity Senescent Shroud Situation Synchronously Tortuous Tranquility Acquiesce Amorous Aroma Awkward Consummate Conversely Deleterious Delirium Ecstasy Enamored Futile Incantation Inevitably Infatuation Inimitable Interminable Intuit Laborious Prosimity Reticence Senescent Shroud Situation Synchronously Tortuous Tranquility Acquiesce Amorous Aroma Awkward Consummate Conversely Deleterious Delirium Ecstasy Enamored Futile Incantation Inevitably Infatuation Inimitable Interminable Intuit Laborious Prosimity Reticence Senescent Shroud Situation Synchronously Tortuous Tranquility Acquiesce Amorous Aroma Awkward Consummate Conversely Deleterious Delirium Ecstasy Enamored Futile Incantation Inevitably Infatuation Inimitable

Joe Pascarell & Ryan Ball of The Machine

THE LETTER

Listening Exercise

Listen to "The Letter" all the way through at least once.
Then listen to the song again, and graffiti up the wall
with any new or unfamiliar words that you hear. Don't
worry if you don't fill up the whole wall . . . we don't
want to have to call a cardiologist!

THE LETTER | Keith Middleton & Rodney Willie | Lyrics by Rodney Willie | Music Written &
Performed by Keith Middleton | Vocals: Avon Marshall | Produced by Keith Middleton |
Technical Producer: Craig Chang

LYRICS

| I wish that we could find a way that we could stay together | I wanna be with you forever | Through calm or **TEMPESTUOUS** weather | (So far away) | Can we go on | I **SURMISE** we both know better | I couldn't let these feelings **FESTER** | So I'm writing you this letter | We've been together the **DURATION** of our high school years | **QUELLED** all our high school fears | Cried all our high school tears | And when our teams played in games we **EXTOLLED** them with the loudest cheers | And when they lost we'd show **DISDAIN** with our other **PEERS** | **EXACTING** homework we'd **COGITATE** on the answers | Studied so late we couldn't stay awake the morning after | Now that it's almost over, I'm more **FORLORN** then I've ever been | I swear I wish we had another year or that school didn't let you in | I wish that we could find a way that we could stay together | I wanna be with you forever | Through calm or **TEMPESTUOUS** weather | (So far away) | Can we go on | I **SURMISE** we both know better | I couldn't let these feelings **FESTER** | So I'm writing you this letter | Now I know I seemed **ELATED** | When you told me that you made it | I tried to **ABSTAIN, REFRAIN** from telling you I hate it | My heart's **DEBILITATED**, don't know if it can handle this | How **IRONIC** that you're going away to become a **CARDIOLOGIST** | Why wasn't I a part of this **COLOSSAL** decision? | Did you not wanna **JEOPARDIZE** our last days with fights and **FRICTION**? | I understand it now but before you leave, one thing you must know | I would've never tried to stop you even though it hurts me so | I'll miss your smile | I'll miss your walk | Your **PANACHE** and style | Our **POIGNANT** talks | Can't believe you're leaving | Please tell me I'm dreaming | Come wake me up | Somebody wake me up | I wish that we could find a way that we could stay together | I wanna be with you forever | Through calm or **TEMPESTUOUS** weather | (So far away) | Can we go on | I **SURMISE** we both know better | I couldn't let these feelings **FESTER** | So I'm writing you this letter (2x) | So far away, so far away | I **SURMISE** we both know better . . .

dic•tion•ar•y

Abstain (v)—refrain, desist; give up; do without. Antonym: indulge (v).
The congressmen abstained from voting on a bill that they did not support.

Cardiologist (n)—physician specializing in the heart and cardiovascular system.
Concerned about his predisposition for heart disease, he made an appointment with a cardiologist.

Cogitate (v)—think, consider, reflect, ponder.
It was necessary to cogitate, given the issue's complexity and importance.

Colossal (adj)—1. gigantic, huge, immense; great size. Antonym: miniscule (adj).
One of the seven wonders of the ancient world, The Colossus of Rhodes was a colossal statue that stood 110 feet tall and took twelve years to complete.

Colossal (adj)—2. important, vital, significant. Antonym: inconsequential (adj).
Former President Truman faced a colossal decision of whether or not to use the atom bomb.

Debilitate (v)—impair, hinder, incapacitate, injure.
He was debilitated by a stroke and now undergoes daily physical therapy.

Disdain (v)—scorn, despise, contempt. Antonym: admire (v).
His ex-girlfriend disdained him.

Duration (n)—period, length; time interval.
The team is toughing it out and digging in for the duration.

Elated (adj)—overjoyed, euphoric, delighted. Antonym: despondent (adj).
She was elated when she found out that she had received a large raise.

Exact (v)—2. take, obtain, demand.
She wanted to exact revenge on the hunter who shot her pet elephant.

Exacting (adj)—1. demanding, challenging. Antonym: easy (adj).
Medical school is exacting because, eventually, you'll be making life-or-death decisions.

Extol (v)—celebrate, praise, commend. Antonym: criticize (v).
The queen's subjects extolled her prosperous reign.

Fester (v)—irritate, aggravate, worsen. Antonym: heal (v).
He said, "You should have a doctor look at that festering boil."

Forlorn (adj)—sad, dejected, lonely, despondent. Antonym: cheerful (adj).
After his girlfriend dumped him, he felt abandoned and forlorn.

Friction (n)—1. resistance, rubbing, abrasion. Antonym: ease (n).
When you apply the car's brakes, the brake pads' friction slows the car.

Friction (n)—2. hostility, antagonism, conflict. Antonym: amity (n).
They always disagreed; whenever they were together, there was friction.

Ironic (adj)—paradoxical, incongruous; describes a surprising outcome in light of an expected result.
I usually carry an umbrella, and ironically, it rained the day I forgot it at home.

Jeopardize (v)—risk, endanger. Antonym: ensure (v).
He didn't want to jeopardize his GPA, so he studied day and night for the final.

Panache (n)—style, élan, confidence, flair. Antonym: inelegance (n).
He has great panache and always wears the finest suits and handmade shoes.

Peer (n)—1. equal, friend, colleague, contemporary, cohort.
The legal system entitles one to be judged by a jury of his or her peers.

Peer (v)—2. gaze, look intently. Antonym: glance (v).
She peered into the candy store window, trying to decide what she wanted.

Poignant (adj)—moving, touching, heartbreaking.
It was a poignant story about a young orphan who is adopted by a loving family.

Quell (v)—allay, alleviate, calm, mitigate.
It was his first time in a helicopter, so the pilot tried to quell his fear of crashing.

Refrain (v)—1. abstain; to avoid doing something. Antonym: indulge (v).
He asked the guy with the cigar, "Would you please refrain from smoking?"

Refrain (n)—2. chorus; a poetic or musical verse that repeats; a repeated excuse.
Democrats blaming Republicans and Republicans blaming Democrats has long been a familiar refrain.

Surmise (v)—deduce, estimate, infer, gather; figure out.
I surmised how big the parking spot was by comparing it to the car adjacent to it.

Tempestuous (adj)—stormy, emotional, passionate. Antonym: calm (adj).
His relationship with his dad is tempestuous and characterized by friction.

I feel the need to **quell** my thirst with something bubbly.

SYNONYM MATCHI♫G

Match the following words with their synonyms. Note the letter of the matching synonym in the space adjacent to the word.

_____ Abstain

_____ Cardiologist

_____ Cogitate   _____ Forlorn

_____ Colossal   _____ Friction

_____ Debilitated   _____ Ironic

_____ Disdain   _____ Jeopardize

_____ Duration   _____ Panache

_____ Elated   _____ Peers

_____ Exacting   _____ Poignant

_____ Extolled   _____ Quell

_____ Fester   _____ Refrain

                      _____ Surmise

                      _____ Tempestuous

(a)	dejected
(b)	touching
(c)	irritate
(d)	risk
(e)	paradoxical
(f)	suppress
(g)	hostility
(h)	contemporaries
(i)	do without
(j)	emotional
(k)	ponder
(l)	challenging
(m)	time interval
(n)	incapacitated
(o)	immense
(p)	abstain
(q)	gather
(r)	heart doctor
(s)	despise
(t)	style
(u)	euphoric
(v)	praise

sentencecompl☺tion

Using a form or tense of the words below, find the one to best complete each of the following sentences.

WORD BANK

Abstain	Exacting	Peers
Cardiologist	Extolled	Poignant
Cogitate	Fester	Quell
Colossal	Forlorn	Refrain
Debilitated	Friction	Surmise
Disdain	Ironic	Tempestuous
Duration	Jeopardize	
Elated	Panache	

1. Choosing between going away to school or attending college locally and living at home is a _____ decision.

2. "I didn't do it" is a familiar _____ of the guilty.

3. Examining the skid marks, the investigator _____ that the driver did not start braking early enough to avoid the accident.

4. He didn't want to let the problem with his sister _____ , so he asked her if they could talk it out.

5. I had a terrible case of the flu and I was completely _____ .

6. Thousands packed the canyon of lower Broadway to _____ John Glenn upon his return as the first American to orbit the Earth.

7. The dean made an impassioned plea for cooler heads to prevail as she tried to _____ the student uprising.

8. Those who perished on 9/11 were remembered in a _____ tribute at the site of the World Trade Center.

9. Talented but _____ , he was difficult to work with if things didn't go his way.

10. Isn't it _____ that "reality" shows are edited?

11. Rivals on the court, they always had _____ between them.

12. My dad had a heart attack and now visits the _____ regularly.

13. Sitting in front of their demolished home, they looked _____ but said that they were happy to have survived the hurricane.

14. Since some students are only comfortable talking about their problems with friends, she started a _____ counseling program at her school.

15. She's a vegetarian and _____ from eating meat.

16. He was _____ by his daughter's safe return from her trek through the Himalayas.

17. The art teacher asked his students to draw cartoons for the _____ of the class and to bring in them in the following week.

18. She _____ him because he was an unrepentant chauvinist.

19. Rolls Royce and Jaguar are established British marques, epitomizing automotive _____ .

20. For centuries philosophers have _____ upon the reason for our existence.

21. If the school doesn't receive additional funding soon, many of its most important programs will be in _____ .

22. Detectives need to be tough and _____ to avoid missing clues.

SYNONYM SENTENCES

In these sentences, use a form or tense of the words below to match their **bolded** synonyms, and write your choice in the space provided following each sentence.

Abstain	Exacting	Peers
Cardiologist	Extolled	Poignant
Cogitate	Fester	Quell
Colossal	Forlorn	Refrain
Debilitated	Friction	Surmise
Disdain	Ironic	Tempestuous
Duration	Jeopardize	
Elated	Panache	

WORD BANK

1. Following a short walk, she said that she was having heart palpitations and that she better see a **doctor**. _____

2. Before I reach a decision, I will need to **think** and consider the relevant data carefully. _____

3. We stood for the **length** of their wedding ceremony, and when it was over I couldn't wait to find a couch to crash on. _____

4. Thunder scares Dakota, so I tried my best to **allay** his fear of the storm. _____

5. Looking at a paw print on the forest path, the ranger said, "From the size of this impression, we can **infer** that this mountain lion was about six feet in length." _____

6. It is **paradoxical** that when she studies exceptionally hard for an exam, she'll usually earn a lower grade than when she studies less intensely. _____

7. These late nights studying are **taking** a toll on me. _____

8. He and his father shared a **touching** moment when they embraced one another for the first time in ten years. _____

9. Her father told her to stop hanging around with the teachers and to spend time with her **friends**. _____

10. While today's movie heroes use brute force to win the day, the leading men of classic movies always succeeded via their wits and **style**. _____

11. He didn't want to **endanger** his chances of getting a car for graduation, so he made sure that he was always home by curfew. _____

12. While putting some new furniture together, I couldn't get one of the nuts to screw onto its bolt, so I put oil on it to reduce the **resistance**. _____

13. Her blister was beginning to **get worse**, so I told her to go see the nurse. _____

14. He was **despondent** over the loss of his puppy and we couldn't cheer him up. _____

15. However, he was **overjoyed** when he got home and his mom told him that she had found the puppy hiding in one of the closets. _____

16. Our coach **praised** the benefits of a healthy diet and regular exercise. _____

17. She also implored us to **abstain** from smoking. _____

18. He said that although the project was a **total** failure, he would get back on his feet and try again. _____

19. Her relationship with her mom is **emotional** because they are so much alike. _____

20. My dad asked my friends to **desist** from eating all of the chocolate in the house every time they came over. _____

21. He treats them with **contempt** whenever they drop by. _____

22. I think he's mentally **impaired**; it's only chocolate. _____

07 The Letter

THE ARTICLE

Read the following article and then, for each question, select the one statement that best describes the author's remarks.

Question 1

(a) The author is guessing that "The Letter" is poignant.

(b) After considering the other tracks on *Vocab Rock,* the author has deduced that "The Letter" is the most touching of all the songs.

(c) Upon his consideration of the songs on *Vocab Rock,* the author has surmised that the poignant vocals on "The Letter" were preformed by Avon Marshall.

(d) Inferring that "The Letter" was written by Keith Middleton and Rodney Willie, the author surmised that the vocals were performed by Avon Marshall.

THE LETTER EXAMINED

NYC—I've surmised that "The Letter" by Keith Middleton and Rodney Willie, with vocals performed by Avon Marshall, is easily the most poignant track on Vocab Rock. The story of a forlorn graduate whose girlfriend has gone off to college to become a cardiologist, Avon describes the irony of the elation of love being debilitated by friction. Their relationship in jeopardy, the graduate cogitates the colossal decision between carrying on for the duration and suffering the toll exacted by his frustration or abstaining from seeing her any longer. Avon's character seems tempestuous; he extols his love's panache but cites a refrain familiar to his peers—that without her near, his longing festers and cannot be quelled. And, as much as he disdains saying so, in the end, he believes it best that they part.—*Keith London*

Question 2

(a) The graduate is despondent because his girlfriend is becoming a doctor but he isn't.

(b) The girlfriend ditched the graduate because he couldn't get into as good a school as she did.

(c) The graduate is forlorn because his girlfriend went off to school to see a cardiologist.

(d) Avon's graduate is dejected because his love went off to study medicine.

Question 3

(a) The singer describes ironing while his elation is debilitated by friction.

(b) It is paradoxical that the euphoria of love can be impaired by conflict.

(c) It is an unexpected outcome that euphoria can be hindered by abrasion.

(d) Avon presents the paradox that an unexpected outcome can be impaired.

Question 4

(a) The couple's love at risk, the graduate ponders his options.
(b) The graduate, being especially bright, has considered how his situation might get him on *Jeopardy!*
(c) The graduate is contemplating how he might jeopardize their relationship.
(d) His girlfriend loves *Jeopardy!*, and he thinks that if he can win, she'll return.

Question 5

(a) The graduate realizes that going on *Jeopardy!* is a big decision.
(b) The graduate is wondering exactly how long their relationship will be at risk.
(c) The graduate wonders whether or not he can endure the frustration of being separated from his girlfriend.
(d) Driving to see his girlfriend, the graduate wonders how long it will take and whether or not there will be any tolls that require exact change.

Question 6

(a) Avon's protagonist reflects on the enormity of deciding whether or not to end their relationship.
(b) The protagonist is pondering how long it will be necessary to refrain from seeing his girlfriend.
(c) Avon's character must go without paying exact tolls for the duration of his drive to see his girlfriend.
(d) All of the above

Question 7

(a) Although he appears emotional, the graduate commends his girlfriend's confidence.
(b) Avon's character is emotional and jealous of his girlfriend's panache.
(c) Extolling élan, Avon's character is overwhelmed with emotion.
(d) The graduate is passionate about his love and praises her flair and sense of style.

Question 8

(a) Citing his girlfriend as the reason, the graduate will avoid being with his colleagues.
(b) The graduate repeats some choruses to his friends.
(c) Avon's character repeats a phrase that his contemporaries would understand.
(d) Avon is going to avoid becoming familiar with his cohorts.

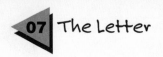

Question 9

(a) The graduate's festering cannot be quelled and he should be seen by a cardiologist right away.

(b) The graduate increasingly misses his girlfriend and he cannot subdue his longing for her.

(c) The graduate is trying to suppress his longing, but he disdains her.

(d) Avon's character has an irritation that needs to be quelled immediately.

Question 10

(a) In the end, the graduate decides to go back to school to earn another degree.

(b) Although he despises saying so, the graduate believes that the end is the best part.

(c) Avon's character is filled with contempt for his girlfriend.

(d) Although it is a difficult decision, the graduate concludes that he and his girlfriend should break up.

UPSIDE DOWN

Listening Exercise

Listen to "Upside Down" all the way through at least once. Then listen to the song again, and graffiti up the wall with any new or unfamiliar words that you hear. Don't worry if you don't fill up the whole wall . . . but how resplendent it would be if you did!

UPSIDE DOWN | Mia Johnson of The Mia Johnson Band | Lyrics by Mia Johnson | Music Written & Performed by Mia Johnson & The Mia Johnson Band | Guitar & Vocals: Mia Johnson | Guitar: Rocco DeCicco | Bass Guitar: Jeff Hiatt | Drums: Tom Walling | Produced by Dave Logan & Craig Chang

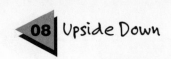

LYRICS

| I'll start where I remember | It was dark and I was driving | In my **PERIPHERAL** a **GLIMMER** | Of headlights on my right side | **DISCONCERTING** all my insides | An **IMPACT** on me broadside | And it now seems I **RESIDE** | Upside down | **GAZING** up to see the ground | Upside down | Everything **INVERTED** all around | **CHAOS** has **INCONTROVERTIBLY** set in | And my luck has gone **SATURNINE** on me again | I **INCURRED** quite a tossing | Overcome by **INCREDULITY** | It took some time after that **JOSTLING** | To regain **EQUANIMITY** | After this **CALAMITY** | **OCCURRING** with such **CELERITY** | A **DEVIANT** reality | Upside down | **GAZING** up to see the ground | Upside down | Everything **INVERTED** all around | **CHAOS** has **INCONTROVERTIBLY** set in | And my luck has gone **SATURNINE** on me again | Despite all of the drama | I was **THAUMATURGICALY UNSCATHED** | Looking up now there's a **PANORAMA** | Of **RESPLENDENT CONSTELLATIONS** | Shining down upon the nations | I have **DEFIED TREPIDATION** | And come out with **JUBILATION** | Cuz I'm no longer | Upside down | **GAZING** up to see the ground | Upside down | Everything **INVERTED** all around | Upside down | Upside down

dic•tion•ar•y

Calamity (n)—disaster, catastrophe, tragedy; event that causes suffering.
The local farmers fear a calamity if the river rises above its banks.
Celerity (n)—swiftness or speed of an action.
Jets travel with great celerity, especially when compared to prop-driven aircraft.
Chaos (n)—confusion; disorder. Antonym: order (n).
The guests couldn't get into the party, the staff was running around trying to find a manager, the DJ didn't show up; it was complete chaos.

Constellation (n)—assemblage; groups of stars that form patterns and have been given names.
In our astronomy class, we studied the constellation the Big Dipper.

Defy (v)—resist, disregard, challenge; refuse to obey.
I would love to fly like a bird and defy gravity.

Deviant (adj)—abnormal; differing from the norm or from socially accepted standards of behavior. Antonym: normal (adj).
What constitutes deviant behavior varies among cultures. For example, here in the United States, it is illegal to marry a relative, whereas in some societies, it is acceptable.

Disconcerting (adj)—disturbing, upsetting, embarrassing. Antonym: comforting (adj).
She has a disconcerting habit of going back on her word.

Equanimity (n)—composure; the state of being calm, even-tempered, level-headed.
She remained calm and maintained her equanimity when she heard of her husband's accident.

Gaze (v)—stare; to look at something intently.
He enjoys gazing out the window at the city below.

Glimmer (v)—shine, gleam, reflect.
Her car glimmered in the sun after she waxed and polished it.

Impact (n)—1. crash, collision.
The meteor's impact created a huge crater in the desert.

Impact (n)—2. influence, impression, effect.
She was a very active volunteer who made a great impact on her community.

Incontrovertibly (adv)—indisputably, unquestionably. Antonym: disputably (adv).
The video playback incontrovertibly shows that she fouled me.

Incredulity (n)—disbelief, skepticism; not able or wanting to believe something. Antonym: conviction (n).
She fought the call and was incredulous, even though the evidence of the foul was on the video playback.

Incur (v)—to bring upon oneself; to sustain an unpleasant outcome; to suffer.
His dad made some stock picks that didn't work out and he incurred huge losses.

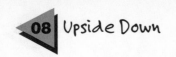

Invert (v)—to turn upside down; to reverse the order of two things. Antonym: righted (v).
At the air show, I watched a stunt plane fly inverted and hoped the pilot's parachute was in working order!

Jostling (v)—shoving, bumping, pushing. Antonym: coddling (v).
With her fans jostling her from every direction, it was hard for the singer to exit the arena.

Jubilation (n)—rejoicing, celebration; an expression of joy. Antonym: sadness (n).
There was jubilation in the crowd when their team won the championship.

Occurring (v)—transpiring; happening.
The movie we saw last night was about a deli clerk who traveled back in time to prevent a calamity from occurring.

Panorama (n)—vista; an unbroken view of a large area.
You can see the panorama of the entire city from the Empire State Building's observation deck.

Peripheral (adj)—tangential, outer, marginal; at the edge. Antonym: central (adj).
During our debate he made points that weren't central to the issue; rather, they were only peripherally related.

Reside (v)—to inhabit; to exist in; to live in a given location.
I plan to study abroad and I'd like to reside in London.

Resplendent (adj)—dazzling, stunning, glorious, brilliant. Antonym: dull (adj).
The vintage aircraft's mirror-polished fuselage was resplendent in the bright sunlight.

Saturnine (adj)—melancholy, gloomy, sullen, glum.
She was saturnine over the loss of her grandmother.

Thaumaturgicaly (adv)—magically, miraculously, supernaturally.
In a story I read, a knight recited an incantation and thaumaturgicaly defeated the dragon.

Trepidation (n)—fear, anxiety, apprehension. Antonym: confidence (n).
Hoping to be accepted with early decision, he opened the envelope from Princeton with trepidation.

Unscathed (adj)—unharmed, intact; without injury or damage. Antonym: damaged (adj).
Astonishingly, she escaped the car accident unscathed.

SYNONYM MATCHI♫G

Match the following words with their synonyms. Note the letter of the matching synonym in the space adjacent to the word.

_____ Calamity

_____ Celerity

_____ Chaos   _____ Incredulous

_____ Constellations   _____ Incur

_____ Defied   _____ Inverted

_____ Deviant   _____ Jostle

_____ Disconcerting   _____ Jubilation

_____ Equanimity   _____ Occur

_____ Gazing   _____ Panorama

_____ Glimmer   _____ Peripheral

_____ Impact   _____ Reside

_____ Incontrovertibly   _____ Resplendent

                               _____ Saturnine

                               _____ Thaumaturgy

                               _____ Trepidation

                               _____ Unscathed

(a)	abnormal
(b)	stare
(c)	sustain
(d)	bump
(e)	live
(f)	disaster
(g)	skeptical
(h)	view
(i)	disregard
(j)	gloomy
(k)	disorder
(l)	dazzling
(m)	celebration
(n)	disturbing
(o)	speed
(p)	magic
(q)	upturned
(r)	assemblage
(s)	gleam
(t)	unharmed
(u)	anxiety
(v)	composure
(w)	outer
(x)	unquestionably
(y)	influence
(z)	transpire

sentencecompl&tion

Using a form or tense of the words below, find the one to best complete each of the following sentences.

WORD BANK

Calamity	Glimmer	Panorama
Celerity	Impact	Peripheral
Chaos	Incontrovertibly	Reside
Constellations	Incredulity	Resplendent
Defied	Incurred	Saturnine
Deviant	Inverted	Thaumaturgy
Disconcerting	Jostling	Trepidation
Equanimity	Jubilation	Unscathed
Gazing	Occurring	

1. He _____ the odds and went on to become a champion.

2. At the concert we _____ our way through the crowd for a position at the foot of the stage.

3. Miraculously, the dog was _____ after being hit by the bike.

4. She often paid her bills after their due date and _____ many late fees as a result.

5. _____ broke out as the agitated crowd was jostled by the stadium ushers.

6. The company was struck by a series of _____ —executive fraud, a massive recall, and a class-action suit—all of which led to its bankruptcy.

7. Sitting on a dune above the beach, he _____ out at the ocean and admired the panorama.

8. She's very calm in difficult situations; you have to respect her _____ .

9. The crowd was _____ as each massive balloon rose out of the staging area and joined the Thanksgiving Day parade.

10. During the nineteenth century it was popular to visit circular exhibit halls that displayed _____ paintings of renowned places or events.

11. Crossing the Golden Gate Bridge on a clear night, you can see the city lights _____ in the distance.

12. Sparkling like a pile of diamonds a hundred miles away, Los Angeles is a _____ beacon.

13. Despite the proof, he was _____ and refused to believe that he was raised by wolves.

14. The _____ of the earth's rotation is 1,070 miles per hour.

15. Humanity's inability to behave humanely is very _____ .

16. The _____ the Big Dipper is a group of stars that looks like a giant pot in the sky.

17. Their prior partnership was very frustrating, so he approached his new collaboration with the artist with some _____ .

18. _____ behavior is not socially acceptable.

19. Her grandparents now _____ in Florida.

20. They were looking for _____ proof of his complicity.

21. A wizard is skilled in _____ .

22. It was awesome; the rollercoaster track turned upside down and _____ the cars as we flew into a sharp turn.

23. A stolid woman, she always wore a _____ expression on her face.

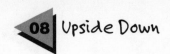

24. Watching a horror movie in a theater, I was scared senseless when I caught something move quickly through my _____ vision.

25. It doesn't matter how many times I reboot my computer, glitches keep _____ .

26. Meteorites hit the moon regularly, leaving its surface pockmarked with _____ craters.

"I've always had a lot of creative **impact** on the music with [producer] Timbaland."
—*Missy Elliot*

SYNONYM SENTENCES

In these sentences, use a form or tense of the words below to match their **bolded** synonyms, and write your choice in the space provided following each sentence.

Calamity	Glimmer	Panorama
Celerity	Impact	Peripheral
Chaos	Incontrovertibly	Reside
Constellations	Incredulity	Resplendent
Defied	Incurred	Saturnine
Deviant	Inverted	Thaumaturgy
Disconcerting	Jostling	Trepidation
Equanimity	Jubilation	Unscathed
Gazing	Occurring	

WORD BANK

1. Her husband better drive with **speed** or she'll have the baby in their car. _____

2. His **sullen** gaze lays bare his life's hardships. _____

3. Not knowing what to expect, she approached the exam with **apprehension**. _____

4. When World War II ended, **celebrating** crowds packed Times Square. _____

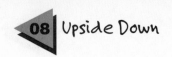

5. For those who reach Mount Everest's summit, it must be sublime to take in the **view** of the entire world below you. _____

6. Remarkably, he was **unharmed** after falling down the stairs. _____

7. The facts prove her statements to be **indisputable**. _____

8. Flying over the shore on a bright summer day, I looked down and saw the beachgoers' sunglasses **shine** like mirrors scattered across the sand. _____

9. Although the Web doesn't appear to have a physical form, it is actually a vast **assemblage** of interconnected computers. _____

10. The protesters **challenged** the government and staged a sit-in near the capital. _____

11. The subway riders **bumped** one another as they made their way out of the crowded station. _____

12. Medieval tales often describe astonishing, **supernatural** events. _____

13. I hate when I bring my car in to be repaired for an intermittent problem and when I get to the shop, it doesn't **happen**. _____

14. He decided to **live** in the city because it was close to his job. _____

15. Her classic 'Vette was **stunning** in bright white livery with blue racing stripes. _____

16. Her mom said, "Stop **staring** out the window and finish your homework!" _____

17. We had so much work to do for the fete that we only took care of the essentials; we blew off doing anything that was **tangential**. _____

18. His house was in a state of complete **disorder** after that party. _____

19. It wouldn't have been such a **catastrophe** if his parents hadn't come back from their vacation early. _____

20. It was pretty **disturbing** to be standing there while they chewed him out. _____

21. They were **in disbelief** that he ignored their instructions not to have anyone over. _____

22. I think what they were most upset about was the **upside-down** ice cream truck in the garage. _____

23. This episode is definitely going to have a huge **effect** on his social life for a few months. _____

24. His dad, who's pretty melodramatic, yelled, "You have **brought upon** my wrath!" _____

25. I can't believe that he handled it all with such **composure**. _____

26. We don't understand what they're so mad about; it's not like he's **abnormal** or anything like that. _____

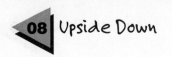
THE ARTICLE

Read the following article, and then, for each question, select the one statement that best describes the author's remarks.

MIA JOHNSON GETS INVERTED

Metro Philly—Artists are always looking for stories to write about, but this tale of chaos came looking for Mia Johnson. I'm jubilant that she's here to tell it, because in this one she almost became a permanent resident of Eternal Rest Acres.

Back on a crystal-clear July night, Mia was driving to a late gig when, in her peripheral vision, she spotted a pair of glimmering headlights rushing toward her. Incredulous, she realized that some deviant ran a stop sign and was about to hit her head on.

Despite her trepidation and the disconcerting image of an imminent calamity, she kept her equanimity, thought with celerity, and stepped on the gas. Bracing herself for what she knew was about to occur, the other car struck her rear wheel directly on the passenger side, and the impact launched her sideways, like a toddler smacking his Hot Wheels with a hockey stick. Flying across the street, driver's-door-first, she hit a fire hydrant on the far side of the road, slamming into it with such force that the car flipped. Then, everything was still.

Opening her eyes, Mia saw that she was inverted, hanging upside down in her seatbelt. Before she unfastened herself, she ran a mental disaster checklist: Pain? Check. Broken bones? Check. Blood? Double check. Defying all probability, she came through thaumaturgical feat, she didn't incur a single scratch, unscathed and just a few bruises. Instead of it being a saturnine moment, it was incontrovertibly one of the best of Mia's life.

She jostled her way out of the seatbelt that saved her life, dropped onto the ceiling, and crawled out through a shattered window. Steeling herself, Mia brought herself to her feet. Confused and startled but intact, she gazed up toward the cosmos and drank in the resplendent panorama of constellations. Safe and thankful to no longer be "Upside Down."—*Keith London*

Question 1

(a) Mia was looking for chaos.

(b) Dr. Chaos was looking for Mia.

(c) A catastrophe was going to befall Mia.

(d) Mia was looking for a story to write about.

Question 2

(a) The author was pleased that Mia was going to be able to get some rest.

(b) Mia is happy that she'll be able to catch some rest.

(c) The author is elated that Mia became a permanent resident.

(d) The author is very happy that Mia did not pass on.

Question 3

(a) On a beautiful summer evening Mia caught a glimpse of a car that was going to hit her.

(b) The oncoming car's headlights were out.

(c) Mia was late to a gig.

(d) She was late getting to a gig, so despite Mia's poor peripheral vision, she was rushing to get there.

Question 4

(a) Mia couldn't believe it when she realized that a deviant was allowed to drive.

(b) She was in a state of disbelief that some joker just ran a stop sign and was about to plow into her.

(c) In a state of disbelief, Mia wondered how the driver of the other car could enjoy a steak while driving.

(d) She could not believe that a law-abiding citizen would pass through a stop sign.

Question 5

(a) Mia is fearful of disturbing images.

(b) She is nervously apprehensive about disconcerting images.

(c) She was fearful of the impending collision.

(d) Mia has trepidation of disconcerting imminent calamities.

Question 6

(a) Despite her trepidation over the disconcerting image, there was an imminent calamity during which she retained her equanimity for celerity.

(b) Despite her anxiety over the imminent accident, Mia stayed level-headed and thought about celery.

(c) In spite of Mia's nervous anxiety regarding the coming collision, she kept her cool, thought with celerity, and stood up in the car.

(d) Despite her fear of the coming collision, she remained level-headed and thought quickly.

Question 7

(a) Mia was wearing braces and she knew that they were going to get hit by the oncoming car.

(b) The oncoming car smashed into her car, throwing it sideways at great speed.

(c) She held herself together, waiting to be struck by a kid with a hockey stick.

(d) The oncoming car smashed into her side, launching the toddler sideways.

Question 8

(a) Her car slid sideways with celerity, smashed into a hydrant, and overturned.

(b) The hydrant flew across the street to flip her car's driver-side door.

(c) Her driver's-side door flew across the street, smashed into the hydrant, and flipped.

(d) After she slid across the street driver-side-first, the hydrant slammed into the car and flipped it.

Question 9

(a) When Mia opened her eyes, she wasn't wearing her seatbelt but she was upside down.

(b) When Mia opened her eyes, she unfastened herself, and then did a disaster check.

(c) When Mia opened her eyes, she was overturned, suspended by her seatbelt.

(d) When Mia opened her eyes, she inverted her mental disaster checklist in her seatbelt.

Question 10

(a) Defying the odds with a magical incantation, she came through unhurt.
(b) Challenging the oncoming car using her supernatural powers, Mia wasn't injured in the crash.
(c) Resisting all probability via some miracle, Mia didn't incur any bruises.
(d) Beating the odds, Mia was miraculously unhurt, incurring only a few bruises.

Question 11

(a) Following the accident, Mia was happy.
(b) After the collision, she was melancholy and sullen.
(c) It was indisputably the most saturnine moment of her life.
(d) Mia's young life is incontrovertibly one of the best.

Question 12

(a) Mia hated wearing her seatbelt and pushed her way out of it.
(b) She shoved her way out of her seatbelt and fell onto the ceiling.
(c) She shattered a window, struggling to get out of her seatbelt.
(d) The shattered glass broke her seatbelt, dropping her onto the ceiling.

Question 13

(a) Delirious but unscathed, Mia admired the stars shimmering in the night sky.
(b) The accident was caused by her drinking problem; she shouldn't have drunk in the constellations.
(c) She is thankful that she no longer needs to drink upside down.
(d) Mia turned into steel and had to drag herself to her feet.

MOVE IT

Listening Exercise

Listen to "Move It" all the way through at least once.
Then listen to the song again, and graffiti up the wall
with any new or unfamiliar words that you hear. Don't
worry if you don't fill up the whole wall . . . it's nothing
to fret about . . .

MOVE IT | F.A.M.E. Ent. | Lyrics by Edmund Blanding & Troy Jackson of F.A.M.E. Ent., with
Keith London | Music Written & Performed by Leon Gaines | Vocals: Troy Jackson | Produced
by Craig Chang

LYRICS

| Let's see if y'all can **GRASP** this clap? | Y'all ready? | We're gonna move it like this | Jump up on it | And clap your hands like this | We're gonna **GAMBOL** like that | Be clear, we here, the party's in the back | I don't wanna **INDUCE** you to do anything you don't wanna do | I'm just that kid that brings **DEVOTION** and a hug or two | I don't wanna commit no **INDISCRETION** | But like I said I just wanna give you the right **IMPRESSION** | We can be **SYMBIOTIC** if our love is forever | If we **BESET** by trouble, we can **RESOLVE** it together | I don't know about **ETERNITY** when starting from scratch | I don't **FRET** or pay attention to the **DISTRACTIONS** in my path | That could be our downfall | What do we need a crowd for | It's just me and you we can paint the town floors | If you're ridin' with me, cool, cause I'm rollin' with you (ok) | Take a pause, girl | Tell me what you wanna do | We're gonna move it like this | Jump up on it and clap your hands like this | We're gonna **GAMBOL** like that | Be clear, we here, the **FETE** is in the back | (2x) | Let's go | Y'all **GRASP** it yet? | Nah, don't worry | We're gonna move on | Let's go | The **CONTEXT** didn't change, but the party's still bumpin' | We in the back with the models, and the convos is comin' | This is a VIP session, you **CAVORTING** or stallin' | Yo' my money got **CLOUT**, so I ain't got no time for spoilin' | So I **RIG** my hat, and brush my shoulders, continue to party | Everything is **EUPHORIC**, as long as we acting properly | If your friend wants to dance, I can dance with two | We can **FROLIC** all night, till the party is through | We're gonna move it like this | Jump up on it and clap your hands like this | We're gonna **GAMBOL** like that | Be clear, we here, the **FETE** is in the back | (2x) | We can party tomorrow | You can party tonight | The after-party's def | What we doin' tonight | (2x) | We're gonna move it like this | Jump up on it and clap your hands like this | We're gonna **GAMBOL** like that | Be clear, we here, the **FETE** is in the back | (2x) | Voice over: "This track is so **SUBLIME**..."

dic•tion•ar•y

Beset (v)—overwhelm, inundate, trouble, harass, surround.
The refugees were beset by one catastrophe after another.
Cavort (v)—jump, horse around, roughhousing; move around in a playful and/or noisy way. Antonym: curtail (v).
Wrestling and tackling each other, the children cavorted on the lawn.
Clout (n)—political power; social or financial influence or importance.
The chairman of the Senate Ethics Committee has enormous clout.
Context (n)—circumstances; details surrounding a subject.
On the news her quote seemed harsh; her remark was actually benign, but it had been taken out of context.
Devotion (n)—dedication, support, commitment. Antonym: indifference (n).
The volunteer's devotion to helping the homeless is inspiring.
Distraction (n)—disturbance, diversion, interruption. Antonym: focus (n).
Listening to music while I work is a distraction.
Eternity (n)—infinity, perpetuity, forever; time without end.
She said that she would love him for all of eternity and would never leave his side.
Euphoric (adj)—overjoyed, elated, exhilarated; greatly happy. Antonym: miserable (adj).
He was euphoric after she accepted his invitation to the concert.
Fete (n)—party, celebration, carnival.
The student union is throwing a fete for the freshmen.
Fret (v)—worry; to be annoyed or anxious. Antonym: relax (v).
He spent the day fretting about the argument he had with his boss.
Frolic (v)—play; to behave in a happy or playful manner. Antonym: grieve (v).
The puppies frolicked in the grass.
Gambol (v)—bound, leap, romp. Antonym: crawl (v).
The dancers gamboled across the stage.
Grasp (v)—1. understand, comprehend. Antonym: misunderstand (v).
The students had a good grasp of some rather difficult material.
Grasp (v)—2. grab, seize. Antonym: release (v).
Struggling to climb into the helicopter, the stuntman grasped the landing skid.

Impression (n)—1. perception, feeling, reaction.
He tried to make a good impression on his girlfriend's mom.
Impression (n)—2. indent, imprint.
She used her thumb to make an impression in the cookie dough.
Indiscretion (n)—carelessness, tactlessness; lack of tact or judgment. Antonym: discretion (n).
The CIA agent who leaked details to the media was fired for his indiscretion.
Induce (v)—persuade, cause; compel using pressure. Antonym: prevent (v).
She tried to induce her daughter to study for her exams.
Resolve (v)—1. solve, decide.
Working together, we can resolve the problem.
Resolve (n)—2. determination, tenacity.
Full of resolve, the stranded mountaineers attempted the treacherous descent.
Rig (v)—fix, arrange, prepare, manipulate.
The competition was rigged by the judges.
Sublime (adj)—awe-inspiring, moving, transcendent, perfect. Antonym: uninspiring (adj).
More than one wine critic has described a favorite vintage as being sublime.
Symbiotic (adj)—describes a mutually beneficial, interdependent relationship. Antonym: parasitic (adj).
In an illustration of the perfect symbiotic relationship, hippos rely on birds to eat flies that would otherwise bite them, and the birds rely on hippos to attract flies, their primary source of food.

SYNONYM MATCHI♫G

Match the following words with their synonyms. Note the letter of
the matching synonym in the space adjacent to the word.

_____ Beset

_____ Cavort

_____ Clout   _____ Frolic

_____ Context   _____ Gambol

_____ Devotion   _____ Grasp

_____ Distraction _____ Impression

_____ Eternity   _____ Indiscretion

_____ Euphoric   _____ Induce

_____ Fete   _____ Resolve

_____ Fret   _____ Rig

               _____ Sublime

               _____ Symbiotic

(a) tactlessness
(b) bound
(c) elated
(d) infinity
(e) influence
(f) understand
(g) pressure
(h) inundated
(i) horse around
(j) disturbance
(k) party
(l) perception
(m) mutually beneficial
(n) transcendent
(o) circumstances
(p) commitment
(q) play
(r) worry
(s) solve
(t) manipulate

sentence**compl**e**tion**

Using a form or tense of the words below, find the one to best complete each of the following sentences.

WORD BANK

Beset	Euphoric	Indiscretion
Cavort	Fete	Induce
Clout	Fret	Resolve
Context	Frolic	Rig
Devotion	Gambol	Sublime
Distraction	Grasp	Symbiotic
Eternity	Impression	

1. She was _____ after finishing the SATs.

2. He couldn't _____ the ideas presented in the article.

3. The neighbor's party was _____ me from my homework.

4. She told him that he needed to _____ the problem today.

5. The _____ to celebrate graduation is being held at my house.

6. He tried to make a good _____ on his girlfriend's parents.

7. In the 1950s Congress investigated game shows that were suspected of being _____ .

8. Taken out of _____ , the senator's sound bite made him appear ridiculous.

9. _____ at the fete, the guys tossed their girlfriends in the pool.

10. His bragging went on and on; it lasted for an _____ .

11. Puppies like to _____ in the open grass.

12. The protesters _____ her to stop wearing fur by telling her about all of the cute little animals that she would save.

13. Edgar Allen Poe, one of English literature's most renowned authors and a tragic figure, was _____ by turmoil during his life and died penniless and alone.

14. Following the revelations of his affair with an intern, former President Clinton became known for his _____ .

15. The dancers _____ across the stage.

16. The queen is regarded as a political figure, although she has no real political _____ .

17. A healthy marriage is a _____ relationship.

18. Man, the beats we heard at the show took you to another place and time; they were _____ .

19. I told him, "Don't sit there _____ about Thursday's exam. Go study!"

20. Martin Luther King _____ his life to achieving racial equality.

SYNONYM SENTENCES

In these sentences, use a form or tense of the words below to match their **bolded** synonyms, and write your choice in the space provided following each sentence.

Beset	Euphoric	Indiscretion
Cavort	Fete	Induce
Clout	Fret	Resolve
Context	Frolic	Rig
Devotion	Gambol	Sublime
Distraction	Grasp	Symbiotic
Eternity	Impression	

WORD BANK

1. The children are **playing** in the yard. _____

2. The street performers **leapt** across the plaza. _____

3. He created a **diversion** while she slipped out the back door. _____

4. My boss says that it doesn't hurt to have friends with **influence**. _____

5. We watched a beautiful sunset the other evening; it was **moving**. _____

6. The kids were **rough-housing** in the backyard. _____

7. He expressed his **commitment** to his girlfriend by proposing. _____

8. Parents often **worry** about their children. _____

9. Although the commercials were only 2 minutes long, it felt as though they went on for an **endless amount of time**. _____

10. Calculus isn't really that hard to **comprehend**. _____

11. After looking at the instructions, I have a pretty good **perception** of what I need to do. _____

12. The two sisters were forced to **solve** their differences. _____

13. He was **overjoyed** after receiving his acceptance letter to law school. _____

14. Urban communities worldwide are **overwhelmed** by air pollution. _____

15. She helped him with his homework, and he helped her with her move; their relationship was **mutually beneficial**. _____

16. If you understand the **circumstances** in which the article was written, its point is clear. _____

17. They **persuaded** him to do the stunt by offering him a pile of cash. _____

18. It is against the law to **manipulate** the lottery. _____

19. Dumb criminals tend to be **careless**, which makes them easy to catch. _____

20. The **party** is at the club on 11th Street and 4th Avenue. _____

THE ARTICLE

Read the following article and then, for each question, select the one statement that best describes the author's remarks.

BLANDING AND JACKSON "MOVE IT"

NYC—Ed Blanding and Troy Jackson of F.A.M.E. Ent. took some time out of their recording schedule to talk with us about their impressive new track, "Move It." Sharing a strong symbiotic relationship, Ed wrote most of the lyrics to "Move It" while Troy is responsible for the track's vocal work. Evidently devoted to their audience, all they want to do is to create music that people will enjoy.

However, the guys thought that writing this song would be easier than it proved to be. Troy remarked, "It took a lot of editing and rigging for us to resolve the problems we confronted while writing this song." Ed added, "One of the most difficult aspects of creating 'Move It' was finding words that fit within the context of the song but were also 'new' words." They didn't fret or let those complications distract them from completing their work, and the guys knew that together they could write a great track that would induce listeners to gambol and cavort to their beats.

We continued our discussion by focusing on the lyrics. Troy and Ed describe "Move It" as a song that should be played at fetes, and it is definitely a track that people can frolic to. Meant to create a euphoric mood, the theme of the song is easily grasped: it's staged at a party where the song's subject is trying to get to know a young lady. "He's being real with the girl, telling her his feelings," states Ed.

Troy and Ed are determined to gain greater exposure in the music industry, and they trust that they won't become beset by the indiscretions that undermine other young artists in this business. They are hopeful that this experience will give them clout to get more recording opportunities, and as musicians, they aspire to continue turning out sublime beats. Oh, and let's not forget that they'd eventually like to become household names, allowing their tracks to live on for eternity. We have their backs...—*Keith London*

Question 1

(a) Ed and Troy have a systematic relationship.
(b) The guys have a mutually beneficial relationship.
(c) "Move It" refers to their management of the recording schedule.
(d) The artists in F.A.M.E. Ent. are concerned about symbiosis.

Question 2

(a) Troy wrote the lyrics and Ed sang.
(b) Ed sang and Troy wrote the lyrics.
(c) They are devoted to enjoying their audience.
(d) It is obvious that they are dedicated to entertaining people.

Question 3

(a) Everyone expects that writing for *Vocab Rock* will be difficult.
(b) The guys wanted to prove themselves.
(c) Troy expressed that it took a lot of effort to write the song.
(d) Ed suggested that they rig the words.

Question 4

   (a) Ed found it hard to find words that fit the circumstances of the song.
   (b) Ed found many good words.
   (c) "Move It" describes what the artists do to words.
   (d) The words they wanted to use were too big to fit into the song.

Question 5

   (a) They were very concerned they weren't up to the task.
   (b) Diversions interfered with their writing.
   (c) Complications distracted them.
   (d) They didn't let anything inhibit the progress of their work.

Question 6

   (a) Ed and Troy wondered if they could write a song that listeners would enjoy.
   (b) They were bounding across the room while they wrote "Move It."
   (c) The guys want to gambol and cavort with listeners.
   (d) They want to get listeners to dance and party.

Question 7

   (a) "Move It' is a song that should be played at feet.
   (b) The guys said that "Move It" is a party track and it fosters an upbeat mood.
   (c) Ed and Troy definitely frolic at parties.
   (d) Frolicking creates euphoria.

Question 8

   (a) The song is set on a stage.
   (b) The subject is grasping a song.
   (c) The theme of "Move It" is easily understood.
   (d) Ed is in a state where he tells girls his feelings.

Question 9

   (a) Ed and Troy want to get into the music industry.
   (b) They are going to suffer from exposure.
   (c) The guys are going to expose the music industry.
   (d) Troy and Ed are determined to expose themselves to music.

Question 10

   (a) The guys are surrounded by the carelessness of other young artists.
   (b) Ed and Troy trust that they won't be as careless as other successful artists.
   (c) Troy and Ed expect that they won't be harassed.
   (d) They trust young artists in the business.

Question 11

   (a) The guys want power.
   (b) Troy and Ed want more chances to record.
   (c) They want the power to record.
   (d) Ed and Troy want more opportunities to obtain recordings.

Question 12

(a) As musicians, they hope to keep beating each other.
(b) They want to turn out to be perfect musicians.
(c) As musicians, Troy and Ed perspire.
(d) The guys want to make great music.

Question 13

(a) They only want to hear their music forever.
(b) Ed and Troy want their names on household products.
(c) The guys would like to eventually have names.
(d) They want their tracks to be enjoyed by audiences forever.

EPHEMERAL DAYS

Listening Exercise

Listen to "Ephemeral Days" all the way through at least once. Then listen to the song again, and graffiti up the wall with any new or unfamiliar words that you hear. Don't worry if you don't fill up the whole wall . . . it's all about the odyssey . . .

EPHEMERAL DAYS | Nina Zeitlin | Lyrics by Nina Zeitlin & Matt Kelly | Written by Nina Zeitlin & Matt Kelly | Vocals & Instrumentation: Nina Zeitlin | Guitar: Rick Briskin | Produced by Dave Logan & Mike Pandolfo

LYRICS

| EPHEMERAL days | Short-lived days | In this **ENIGMATIC HAZE** | I can't even **APPRAISE** | A **CACOPHONY** of feelings | In a **CAPTIVATING** place | I can't **SURVEY** this city | 'Cause I'll be gone without a trace | I had a **VAGUE CONCEPTION** | Of what I might **PERCEIVE** | I knew it'd be **BEATIFIC** | Didn't realize I'd never want to leave | Took a plane to Barcelona | **AMBLED** down the streets | The **ANTIQUITY INTRIGUED** me | I felt **LICENTIOUS** as I thought about the people I could meet | **EMBARKING** on this **SOJOURN** | An **ODYSSEY** it would be | **FLAGRANTLY ELATED** | Can't **DISSUADE** me **ERRONEOUSLY** | I had a **VAGUE CONCEPTION** | Of what I might **PERCEIVE** | I knew it'd be **BEATIFIC** | Didn't realize I'd never want to leave (yeah) | Surrounded by **NOVELTY** | The **PROFUSION** of what might be | **CONFOUNDED** by **MODESTY** | And what it could **IMPART** to me | The city **ENDURES** forever | But I can't **LINGER**, I have to **ABSCOND** | I can't **PROLONG** my time here | So tomorrow I'll be moving on | **EPHEMERAL** Days | Short-lived days (Hmm) | As I **SOLEMNLY** gaze | I know I'll be back someday (yeah) | **EPHEMERAL** Days | Yeah

dic•tion•ar•y

Abscond (v)—escape, leave; depart secretly.
  They didn't want their wedding to turn into the circus that their parents were planning, so they absconded to Las Vegas to elope.
Amble (v)—stroll, wander, mosey. Antonym: run (v).
  I ambled down the city streets, stopping now and then to window shop.
Antiquity (n)—ancient times, or a relic of ancient times; old age.
  Rome, Italy not only dates to antiquity, but it is also filled with antiquities.
Appraise (v)—evaluate, price, assess, assay.
  She brought her ring to the jeweler to be appraised.

Beatific (adj)—good, innocent, virtuous. Antonym: sinister (adj).
Mother Theresa led a beatific life caring for the impoverished.
Cacophony (n)—noise, din. Antonym: silence (n).
While we were camping, the cacophony of crickets chirping kept us awake.
Captivating (adj)—entrancing, charming, enthralling. Antonym: repellent (adj).
He found the ancient city captivating.
Conception (n)—1. beginning, outset. Antonym: conclusion (n).
From its conception, all of us recognized that the idea was a stroke of genius.
Conception (n)—2. idea, notion.
Late again, it was obvious that she had no conception of time.
Confound (v)—confuse, puzzle, perplex, baffle. Antonym: clarify (v).
The directions confounded him, so he was unable to use the DVD player.
Dissuade (v)—deter, discourage. Antonym: encourage (v).
Her boss tried to dissuade her from quitting.
Elated (adj)—overjoyed, euphoric, delighted. Antonym: despondent (adj).
She was elated when she found out that she had received a large raise.
Embark (v)—leave, commence; begin a journey or some undertaking; board a boat or airplane.
A frequent literary theme involves characters embarking upon on a journey for one reason or another.
Endure (v)—1. persist; exist for an extended period of time.
Great classical compositions have endured the test of time.
Endure (v)—2. to bear; tolerate.
She said that she couldn't endure another moment of his lunacy, and then she left him.
Enigmatic (adj)—mysterious, inscrutable; difficult to understand.
Never an easy person to categorize, I always regarded him as enigmatic.
Ephemeral (adj)—short-lived; fleeting, brief.
After saving the baby from the fire, he had his "15 minutes of fame," but he knew that all of the attention would be ephemeral.
Erroneously (adv)—incorrectly, mistakenly.
The New York Post *erroneously reported that Dick Gephardt was the Democratic vice presidential candidate in the 2004 presidential election.*

10 Ephemeral Days

Flagrantly (adv)—conspicuously, blatantly, brazenly. Antonym: modestly (adv).
He strode down the hall, flagrantly flashing his new gold bracelet.

Haze (n)—fog, mist; anything airborne that inhibits one's ability to see.
After the brushfire was extinguished, a smoky haze lingered in the air for days.

Impart (v)—tell, grant, reveal, communicate; pass on information.
I enjoy being a mentor and imparting knowledge to other people.

Intrigued (v)—interested, curious. Antonym: disinterested (v).
He was intrigued by their suggestion that they might buy his company.

Licentious (adj)—immoral, lewd, unrestrained. Antonym: modest (adj).
The bouncer kicked him out of the club because of his licentious behavior.

Linger (v)—loiter, persist, hang around.
The cataclysmic events of 9/11 will linger in the minds of Americans forever.

Modesty (n)—reserve, humility, discretion. Antonym: arrogance (n).
She contributes to many charities, but her modesty precludes her from discussing it.

Novelty (n)—newness, uniqueness.
Once the novelty of their new toy wore off, the children lost interest in it.

Odyssey (n)—a long, eventful journey.
The novel I'm reading follows an adopted woman's odyssey to find her biological parents.

Perceive (v)—discern, recognize, notice. Antonym: ignore (v).
Catching a glimpse of the blue car in his rearview mirror again, he perceived that he was being followed.

Profusion (n)—overabundance, surplus, excess, many; large number or amount. Antonym: dearth (n).
The television station received a profusion of calls about the anchorperson's inflammatory remarks.

Prolong (v)—extend, lengthen; draw out; usually associated with time. Antonym: curtail (v).
We enjoyed our trip to Madrid so much that we decided to prolong our stay for three more days.

Sojourn (n)—visit; temporary stay.
Unfortunately, since I was on my way to London for business, my sojourn in Paris was quite brief.

Solemnly (adv)—seriously, gravely. Antonym: merrily (adv).

The news anchorperson solemnly described the events that led to the tragic fire.

Survey (v)—review, analyze.

Flying over the remains of the smoldering brushfire, the ranger surveyed the damage to the forest.

Vague (adj)—unclear, indistinct. Antonym: clear (adj).

I have a vague memory of the cousins who I met six years ago.

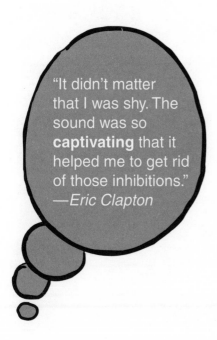

"It didn't matter that I was shy. The sound was so **captivating** that it helped me to get rid of those inhibitions."
—*Eric Clapton*

SYNONYM MATCHI♪G

Match the following words with their synonyms. Note the letter of the matching synonym in the space adjacent to the word.

_____ Abscond

_____ Ambled

_____ Antiquity   _____ Flagrantly

_____ Appraise   _____ Haze

_____ Beatific   _____ Impart

_____ Cacophony   _____ Intrigued

_____ Captivating   _____ Licentious

_____ Conception   _____ Linger

_____ Confounded   _____ Modesty

_____ Dissuade   _____ Novelty

_____ Elated   _____ Odyssey

_____ Embark   _____ Perceive

_____ Endure   _____ Profusion

_____ Enigmatic   _____ Prolong

_____ Ephemeral   _____ Sojourn

_____ Erroneously   _____ Solemnly

      _____ Survey

      _____ Vague

(a)	mist
(b)	newness
(c)	unclear
(d)	reserve
(e)	escape
(f)	visit
(g)	tell
(h)	begin
(i)	ancient time
(j)	fleeting
(k)	noise
(l)	mysterious
(m)	journey
(n)	wrongly
(o)	strolled
(p)	loiter
(q)	curious
(r)	review
(s)	overjoyed
(t)	evaluate
(u)	persist
(v)	seriously
(w)	overabundance
(x)	virtuous
(y)	notion
(z)	discourage
(a1)	extend
(a2)	notice
(a3)	immoral
(a4)	entrancing
(a5)	blatant
(a6)	perplexed

sentencecompletion

Using a form or tense of the words below, find the one to best complete each of the following sentences.

WORD BANK

Abscond	Confounded	Flagrantly	Odyssey
Ambled	Dissuade	Haze	Perceive
Antiquity	Elated	Impart	Profusion
Appraise	Embarking	Intrigued	Prolong
Beatific	Endures	Licentious	Sojourn
Cacophony	Enigmatic	Linger	Solemnly
Captivating	Ephemeral	Modesty	Survey
Conception	Erroneously	Novelty	Vague

1. He had the painting _____ and was surprised to learn that it was very valuable.

2. It is easy to see (and hear) how the _____ of sounds in a big city can overwhelm some people.

3. Pablo Picasso, a painter who often portrayed people's eyes on the same side of their heads, is known for his _____ style.

4. Her _____ smile is angelic.

5. The _____ made it difficult for the driver to see what was ahead.

6. They _____ for the Bahamas via JFK International Airport.

7. We decided to _____ our date by going dancing after we saw the movie.

8. She _____ believed that she would pass English, but she'll be retaking the class during summer school.

9. The professor _____ some of his accumulated wisdom to the class.

10. Although my friend felt he would wind up flipping burgers, the principal was determined to _____ him from dropping out.

11. After the doctors told her that she had six months to live, she _____ them by overcoming her illness.

12. I _____ down the beach, stopping occasionally to pick up seashells.

13. Sometimes, it's the _____ nature of summer relationships that makes them work.

14. I saw an animated cat-and-mouse flick that _____ ripped off some classic cartoons.

15. The painting was so beautiful that I couldn't take my eyes off of it; it was _____ .

16. Skulking through the alleyway, the jewel thieves _____ with the gems they stole.

17. It is extraordinary that William Shakespeare's works continue to _____ century after century.

18. She was very demure, and her _____ prevented her from talking about her achievements.

19. He had never encountered such a device before and was _____ by its novelty.

20. She got lost on her way here because the directions were too _____ .

21. Recognizing that it was futile to try following the vague directions, she said, "Well, I have no _____ of how to get there."

22. After my friend opened a ketchup bottle by using his belly button, I said, "Well, that was certainly a _____ approach."

23. The readers _____ recited the names of those who lost their lives in the fire.

24. Before we rented a tent for the party, I went out to _____ the backyard to determine out how it would best fit.

25. It was one of those great ephemeral love affairs—two people meeting one another during a brief _____ , enjoying each other's company, and then continuing on their separate paths.

26. Las Vegas, which is known as "Sin City," is playing up its _____ image to attract tourists.

27. Opening the stereo cabinet, I found a _____ of wires and realized that I had no idea what I was doing.

28. The Pyramids in Giza, Egypt, date to _____ .

29. Trying to get her laptop fixed, she spoke with four customer service reps, three different technicians, and a software engineer; it was an

_____ .

30. I may be wrong, but they look like they're up to no good, just _____ in the hallway, furtively looking back and forth.

31. If they're supposed to be in the building, I _____ that they may be waiting for someone to come with the keys to the apartment.

32. She was _____ when she found out that she had won the car.

SYNONYM SENTENCES

In these sentences, use a form or tense of the words below to match their **bolded** synonyms, and write your choice in the space provided following each sentence.

Abscond	Confounded	Flagrantly	Odyssey
Ambled	Dissuade	Haze	Perceive
Antiquity	Elated	Impart	Profusion
Appraise	Embarking	Intrigued	Prolong
Beatific	Endures	Licentious	Sojourn
Cacophony	Enigmatic	Linger	Solemnly
Captivating	Ephemeral	Modesty	Survey
Conception	Erroneously	Novelty	Vague

WORD BANK

1. He wanted to **evaluate** the situation before deciding what to do. _____

2. Despite her great wealth she was a very **reserved**, understated person. _____

3. I haven't lived in Paris for years, but the memories of my time there **persist**. _____

4. Getting this company started has been an **arduous journey**. _____

5. At the earliest opportunity, the wife and I are going for a quick **visit** to South Beach. _____

6. She wanted to tan, but a light **fog** was blocking the sun. _____

7. When he knocked over all of the pots that had been drying, his mom, jarred by the sound of crashing cookware, yelled, "What is that **noise**?" _____

8. Despite his efforts to get her to leave for someplace safe, he couldn't **deter** her from staying. _____

9. We looked at the photo she took of what she told us was the Loch Ness Monster, but all we could make out was the **unclear** outline of something in the water. _____

10. Slipping into the night, the spies **escaped** with a copy of the secret launch codes. _____

11. The burlesque dancers **lewdly** draped themselves over the show's host. _____

12. In a low, **serious** voice, the doctor informed her that her condition was inoperable. _____

13. With roots that reach back thousands of years, the world's major religions all date to **ancient times**. _____

14. I was too excited to sleep because today we're **leaving** on our journey. _____

15. He's been working on the project for years but it was originally her **idea**. _____

16. After their argument, she **mistakenly** believed that he would wait for her. _____

17. I love to **wander** through interesting parts of the city that I don't know yet. _____

18. Given that his car was gone, I **recognized** that he had already left. _____

19. I was intrigued by the **newness** of the technology. _____

20. The recording star **puzzled** her critics by becoming more popular than ever. _____

21. He was **euphoric** when he received his acceptance letter from MIT. _____

22. After the tornado she came out of the cellar to **review** the damage to the house. _____

23. On our trek through the Amazon, a native priest **revealed** his wisdom to us. _____

24. Poetry has always been **mysterious** to her, and she can never figure out what the author is trying to say. _____

25. The new technology was **interesting** and sparked my curiosity. _____

26. Lazy summer days are always too **fleeting**. _____

27. I did everything I could to **extend** my afternoon nap on Sunday, but the din outside kept waking me up. _____

28. There is a **surplus** of diet gimmicks on the market, but that doesn't mean that any of them work. _____

29. Dakota is the cutest little kid with the most **innocent** smile. _____

30. I urged her to stay inside where it was safe, but she **blatantly** ignored my advice and walked out into the hurricane. _____

31. I always like to **hang around** after a movie ends to see if the director did anything interesting during the credits, like include intriguing outtakes. _____

32. She was **entranced** by the film's lush imagery. _____

THE ARTICLE

Read the following article and then, for each question, select the one statement that best describes the author's remarks.

NINA ZEITLIN'S "EPHEMERAL DAYS"

NYC—While lingering at Native we had a chance to speak with the beatific Nina Zeitlin, the artist who composed and performs "Ephemeral Days."

Her second track for *Vocab Rock*, she conceived the title before she had written the song. The really peculiar part is that it came to Nina just because she was intrigued by the word "ephemeral," which means "fleeting" or "short-lived." Fortuitously, while cruising Europe on vacation, she began to appraise the track's lyrics on her way to Barcelona, Spain, and as a result, the song imparts many of the experiences she had on her odyssey.

Surveying the city, Nina found Barcelona a novel, captivating place, and was in awe at its antiquity. Elated to embark on this sojourn, she was impressed by the flagrant architecture, with which she had a vague familiarity before she arrived. And, accustomed to the bravado of New Yorkers, Nina was confounded by Barcelona's similar profusion of cultures, but struck by the modesty of its inhabitants. Expecting the same dynamic, given the city analogous circumstances, she found the city enigmatic.

Erroneously expecting this trip to be just another vacation, Nina fell in love with Barcelona as she ambled licentiously through the city's cacophonous streets. Although she wished she could have prolonged her journey, her life back home dissuaded her from staying. Departing was the most solemn aspect of her travels, and despite her desire to remain there, she had to abscond, or as she says, she "might have stayed for good." Barcelona's impact on Nina can't be appraised, but she perceives that however hazy her memories become, they will no doubt endure.—*Rebecca Osleeb*

Question 1

(a) The authors are studio malingerers.
(b) The authors were lingering around natives.
(c) The authors are recording natives in a studio.
(d) The authors were hanging around the production studio.

Question 2

(a) Nina conceived her second song for *Vocab Rock* before she thought of a title.
(b) The title "Ephemeral Days" is beautifully conceived.
(c) She thought of the title prior to writing the song.
(d) None of the above

Question 3

(a) Nina likes a word that means "short-lived."
(b) *Ephemeral* is a peculiar word.
(c) "Ephemeral Days" has some peculiar verses.
(d) Peculiar parts came to Nina.

Question 4

(a) She evaluated the lyrics while on a cruise ship to Barcelona, Spain.
(b) Nina was on vacation when she began writing the lyrics.
(c) Her odyssey brought her to forts throughout Europe.
(d) On her way to Barcelona, Nina had many experiences.

Question 5

(a) Ideas and words for the song were written at different times.
(b) Writing "Ephemeral Days" was an odyssey.
(c) She copied parts of *The Odyssey* to write her song.
(d) "Ephemeral Days" is about days being shorter in Barcelona.

Question 6

(a) She found the city magnificent and rich in history.
(b) She was captured in Barcelona while she was measuring it.
(c) Nina found a city book and was struck by its age.
(d) Nina wrote a novel about the city's antiquity.

Question 7

(a) Her flagrance was familiar and impressive.
(b) Nina was happy to bark on her sojourn.
(c) She was excited to begin her visit.
(d) She disembarked to find vague architecture.

Question 8

(a) Barcelona's wild architecture was vague, yet familiar to her.
(b) Nina had a modest knowledge of the city's outstanding architecture.
(c) Barcelona, notable for its flagrant architects, is a beautiful city.
(d) Nina was impressed by the flagrant architects she knew.

Question 9

(a) Her New York bravado confounded the city's modest inhabitants.
(b) She was struck by the multiplicity of cultures and the restraint of its citizens.
(c) Accustomed to New Yorkers, she found too many cultures in Barcelona.
(d) New Yorkers' outgoing nature confuses Nina.

Question 10

(a) Nina expected to be mystified by Barcelona's circumstances.
(b) The analogous dynamics of the cities' circumstances were enigmatic.
(c) Compared to New York, she found Barcelona difficult to understand.
(d) Accustomed to New York, the uniformity of Barcelona's cultures mystified her.

Question 11

(a) Nina made a mistake assuming that she would be on vacation.
(b) She wandered through the city looking for trouble.
(c) Barcelona's noisy streets caused her to make errors.
(d) Nina was captivated by Barcelona and savored walking its bustling streets.

Question 12

(a) Nina would have liked to stay in Barcelona, but she needed to get home.
(b) Her friends talked her out of extending her journey.
(c) Barcelona's beauty dissuaded her from prolonging her journey.
(d) Her trip was prolonged by her life back home in New York.

Question 13

(a) She absconded from Barcelona under the solemn cover of night.
(b) Nina was sad to leave Barcelona, but she was compelled to do so.
(c) The authorities didn't like Nina's lingering, so she had to abscond.
(d) Despite her tendency to linger, her travels were solemn.

Question 14

(a) However perceptive she may be, Nina cannot appraise her impact on Barcelona.
(b) Nina believes that Barcelona will make her memory hazy.
(c) Her enduring memories cannot be appraised because they are hazy.
(d) She expects that she will remember Barcelona for an indefinite period.

mia Johnson

SUBLIME

Listening Exercise

Listen to "Sublime" all the way through at least once. Then listen to the song again, and graffiti up the wall with any new or unfamiliar words that you hear. Don't worry if you don't fill up the whole wall . . . but scurry along 'cause we don't have all day!

SUBLIME | Joe Pascarell & The Machine | Lyrics by Joe Pascarell | Music Written & Performed by Joe Pascarell & The Machine | Guitar: Joe Pascarell | Bass Guitar & Vocals: Ryan Ball | Drums: Todd Cohen | Produced by Joe Pascarell

LYRICS

| I was LANGUID in my GAIT | I was BARREN in my heart | I would MUDDLE through the day | BERATING everything | DELUDED by the HOAX | Of an APATHETIC STATE | Then your IRIDESCENT smile | Took me to a life SUBLIME | I'm a PALPITATING mess | When I'm around you | And I'm losing my FINESSE | And I'm BASKING in the glow | Now I QUIVER like a child | 'Cause I've found you | VINDICATE me with your smile | Let it SHIMMER all inside | Now I'm drinking in the DIN of the RANDOM song of life | As I SCURRY to your home | I can SAVOR what's around | And as I UNRAVEL you | And you SUCCUMB to me | We can live this LUCID dream | We can live a life SUBLIME | I'm a PALPITATING mess | When I'm around you | And I'm losing my FINESSE | And I'm BASKING in the glow | Now I QUIVER like a child | 'Cause I've found you | VINDICATE me with your smile | Let it SHIMMER all inside | I'm a PALPITATING mess | When I'm around you | And I'm losing my FINESSE | And I'm BASKING in the glow | Now I QUIVER like a child | 'Cause I've found you | VINDICATE me with your smile | Let it SHIMMER all inside

dic•tion•ar•y

Apathetic (adj)—indifferent, uninterested. Antonym: enthusiastic (adj).
You can't be apathetic about going to war.

Barren (adj)—desolate, sterile, unproductive. Antonym: fertile (adj).
Barren and inhospitable, the Sahara Desert's average rainfall is less than 5 inches annually and daytime temperatures can reach 130 degrees Fahrenheit.

Bask (v)—luxuriate, lie, sunbathe; take pleasure in warmth or lying in the sun.
Being cold-blooded, lizards like to bask in the sun.

Berate (v)—rebuke, criticize, scold, chastise. Antonym: encourage (v).
She berated him for not making an effort to do a good job.

Delude (v)—deceive, con, mislead.
She's deluding herself if she thinks that she'll get a recording contract because she's completely tone-deaf.

Din (n)—noise, racket. Antonym: tranquility (n).
When I'm in the city, the din of rumbling trucks, sirens, and people makes it impossible to sleep.

Finesse (n)—skill, poise. Antonym: clumsiness (n).
Placing each part in the tiny case with great care, the watchmaker demonstrated extraordinary finesse when he was repairing my Rolex.

Gait (n)—pace; manner of walking or running.
My father was hurt when he was a child and now walks with an uneven gait.

Hoax (n)—trick, practical joke.
He was infuriated to discover that his mansion had been burglarized, but then he was relieved to find out that his friends were just playing a hoax.

Iridescent (adj)—glowing, gleaming.
Her new cell phone lights up and gives off an iridescent glow when it rings.

Languid (adj)—relaxed, unhurried, lethargic. Antonym: harried (adj).
The audience was bored by the languid pace of the speaker's presentation.

Lucid (adj)—coherent, comprehensible, intelligible; clearly understood. Antonym: incoherent (adj).
After a baseball hit the player in the head, the paramedic wanted to make sure that he was lucid.

Muddle (v)—to behave in a confused or disorderly manner; jumbled.
She didn't know her lines in the play and muddled through the performance.

Palpitate (v)—throb, flutter.
On our first date I was so nervous my heart was palpitating.

Quiver (v)—tremble, shake.
She was so scared that she began to quiver.

Random (adj)—haphazard; by chance. Antonym: systematic (adj).
He didn't care what color notebook he bought and just picked one at random.

11 Sublime

Savor (v)—relish, appreciate, enjoy.
Prepared by one of the city's finest chefs, she savored every bite of her meal.

Scurry (v)—scamper, dash; move briskly. Antonym: amble (v).
When it was time for his bubble bath, he scurried up the stairs to the tub.

Shimmer (v)—twinkle, glint; shine intermittently.
The moonlight shimmered on the surface of the lake.

State (v)—1. assert; to declare.
She stated that she wasn't going to tolerate his idiocy any longer and left him.

State (n)—2. condition, circumstances; frame of mind.
He was such a slob, his mom couldn't believe the state of his room.

State (n)—3. territory, nation, country.
The secretary of state represents the United States in the world forum.

Sublime (adj)—awe-inspiring, perfect, transcendent. Antonym: uninspiring (adj).
The orchestra's performance was the finest I've ever heard; it was sublime.

Succumb (v)—yield, die, submit; give way, give in.
Eve succumbed to the temptation of the forbidden fruit.

Unravel (v)—disentangle, untangle, solve; work loose.
Losing his supporters one by one, his plan began to unravel.

Vindicate (v)—justify, support, exonerate; clear of blame.
The company's profits vindicated the CEO's unorthodox management style.

SYNONYM MATCHI♫G

Match the following words with their synonyms. Note the letter of the matching synonym in the space adjacent to the word.

_____ Apathetic

_____ Barren

_____ Basking

_____ Berate

_____ Deluded

_____ Din

_____ Finesse

_____ Gait

_____ Hoax

_____ Iridescent

_____ Languid

_____ Lucid

_____ Muddled

_____ Palpitating

_____ Quiver

_____ Random

_____ Savor

_____ Scurry

_____ Shimmer

_____ State

_____ Sublime

_____ Succumb

_____ Unravel

_____ Vindicate

(a) twinkle
(b) skill
(c) jumbled
(d) desolate
(e) relaxed
(f) yield
(g) trick
(h) scold
(i) disentangle
(j) indifferent
(k) coherent
(l) sunbathing
(m) scamper
(n) perfect
(o) glow
(p) condition
(q) noise
(r) pace
(s) relish
(t) haphazard
(u) shake
(v) deceived
(w) throbbing
(x) exonerate

sentencecompl@tion

Using a form or tense of the words below, find the one to best complete each of the following sentences.

WORD BANK

Apathetic	Hoax	Savor
Barren	Iridescent	Scurry
Basking	Languid	Shimmer
Berating	Lucid	State
Deluded	Muddle	Sublime
Din	Palpitating	Succumb
Finesse	Quiver	Unravel
Gait	Random	Vindicate

1. Looking down at the street from my office window, I watched the people _____ as the rain began to fall.

2. She _____ him for telling her that aliens stole his homework.

3. Questioning him, she thought that his story would _____ .

4. Positive that his tale was a _____ , she sent him to the principal.

5. Then, all of a sudden, an unusual light with an _____ glow came through the window.

6. We couldn't believe our eyes, but a tall figure that _____ in the light stepped in through the window and handed the teacher his homework.

7. _____ by the extraordinary events, he came back to the classroom and said, "I told you that aliens stole my homework!"

8. After a great day of swimming and basking in the sun, we ambled down the beach at a _____ pace to head back to our hotel.

9. My grandfather was sent to the hospital with heart _____ .

10. The Confederate army _____ to Union forces in March 1865.

11. When I go to the beach, all I want to do is _____ in the sun.

12. Photographs of Mars depict a _____ , rocky landscape.

13. As the bear slowly approached us, we began to _____ with fear.

14. Unable to finish a sentence, it was obvious that her thoughts were _____ .

15. After sampling a very fine vintage bottle of wine, the connoisseur remarked, "What a _____ finish!"

16. Never having encountered such an extraordinary vintage before, he _____ every drop.

17. His mom said, "He is completely _____ if he expects me to pick up after him for the rest of his life."

18. We cannot become _____ and take democracy for granted.

19. I couldn't keep up with my sister as we walked downtown because she has a much longer _____ than I do.

20. He gave a clear and _____ argument supporting states' rights.

21. The speaker was forced to yell over the _____ of the crowd.

22. After 9/11 it isn't uncommon to be subjected to a _____ search at an airport.

23. But, I'm sad to say, that is today's _____ of affairs.

24. He forgot her name, but handled the situation with such
_____ that she was happy to excuse the gaffe.

Don't **delude** me . . . does this balloon make me look fat?

SYNONYM SENTENCES

In these sentences, use a form or tense of the words below to match their **bolded** synonyms, and write your choice in the space provided following each sentence.

Apathetic	Hoax	Savor
Barren	Iridescent	Scurry
Basking	Languid	Shimmer
Berating	Lucid	State
Deluded	Muddle	Sublime
Din	Palpitating	Succumb
Finesse	Quiver	Unravel
Gait	Random	Vindicate

WORD BANK

1. She only slept for a few hours last night and woke up completely **confused** this morning. _____

2. Her beautiful hair **glinted** in the sunlight. _____

3. He found the hose in knots but **untangled** it so he could water the plants. _____

4. It was an elaborate **practical joke**, which took months to prepare. _____

5. Cold-blooded animals need to **lie** in the sun to maintain their body temperatures. _____

6. Acquitted by the jury, the defendant was thrilled to be **exonerated**. _____

7. During hot, humid summer days, I like to keep a **relaxed** pace. _____

8. He lacked **skill**, but he always got the job done. _____

9. Sometimes, given the overwhelming crises here at home, it's hard not to be **indifferent** about problems elsewhere. _____

10. The horse trainer was irate when he found out that the mare he just bought was **sterile**. _____

11. As the Grammy results were read, she **shook** with anticipation. _____

12. Following her fall down the stairs, he asked her how many fingers he was holding up to see if she was **coherent**. _____

13. The mouse **dashed** across the kitchen floor. _____

14. The **noise** of the traffic kept me awake all night. _____

15. There is something **transcendent** about every morning's sunrise. _____

16. I'm always in awe of the sun's **glow** as it breaches the horizon. _____

17. The horse trotted at a moderate **pace**. _____

18. To me, events seem pretty **haphazard**, and—good or bad—you never know what's going to happen next. _____

19. After he found out that he she conned him, he said, "I can't believe that I was so **misled**!" _____

20. My heart was **throbbing** after the 4-mile run. _____

21. The teacher **rebuked** her for coming late to class. _____

22. When he awoke in an unfamiliar place, he was in a very confused **frame of mind**. _____

23. Exhausted from battling the disease for years, my grandmother **gave in** and passed away this morning. _____

24. Great achievements are always comprised of small feats, so I **relish** every accomplishment, no matter how insignificant it might seem. _____

THE ARTICLE

Read the following article and then, for each question, select the one statement that best describes the author's remarks.

THE "SUBLIME" PIECE

NYC—Scurrying into Native's doorway to get in from the rain, I was having heart palpitations from my mad, six-block dash to escape a sudden deluge. It was coming down in buckets. Basking in the reflection of the iridescent bulb overhead, its outline shimmered in the droplets clinging to my coat. There's something sublime about standing just out of the rain and watching New York come to a halt as the sky opens up on a summer afternoon.

For a minute, I deluded myself into believing that the downpour was going to end quickly, as I thought of grabbing a quick cup of coffee before I went up to the studio. I succumbed to the fact that it was not going to happen and I headed upstairs. I was lucid, but my pace was languid, and I was feeling pretty apathetic. Everything was cool, but it was just one of those random days when your brain is muddled, and you've lost all of your finesse. Sometimes you think your friends are playing a hoax on you, but unfortunately, that's almost never the case and your day continues to unravel.

But, then again, there are days when your endurance is vindicated. As I exited the elevator and stepped into the loft, I entered a different state. There were some excellent tracks coming out of the studios, and I savored another day among some very talented people making great music. A bit of life returned to my gait, and I quivered for a second when through the din, I heard Adrienne Hecker hit some incredibly high note. I berated myself for letting the rain get the best of me and then went to the kitchen to see if there was any coffee I could make. Of course, the cabinet was barren. Man, I knew I should have grabbed a cup when I was downstairs...—Keith London

Question 1

(a) The article is written from the perspective of a small, scurrying animal.

(b) The author was running to get out of the rain and couldn't catch his breath.

(c) There was a flood in New York that the author was trying to escape.

(d) The author is a jogger who enjoys running in the rain.

Question 2

(a) The doorway light cast a glow that twinkled in the raindrops on the author's jacket.

(b) The author wanted to bask in the sun in front of the studio.

(c) Lightbulbs were clinging to the author's coat and were casting a shimmering light in the rain.

(d) The raindrops were reflecting the author's coat while he was basking in the doorway.

Question 3

(a) The author finds perfection standing in the rain on a summer day in New York.
(b) Keith likes to watch for the perfect rain, which can only be spotted from doorways.
(c) The author would like it to rain more often because it brings New York to a standstill.
(d) He savors the odd tranquility that occurs when it rains heavily in New York.

Question 4

(a) Keith is deluding himself that he can go to the studio without coffee.
(b) The author was delusional regarding his ability to stop the rain.
(c) He was kidding himself when he thought that the rain would stop soon.
(d) The author likes to grab coffee, but it needs to be made quickly.

Question 5

(a) He yielded to not getting coffee upstairs.
(b) Keith gave in to the fact that the rain was not going to let up.
(c) The author thought there was coffee upstairs and decided not to bring any.
(d) He died in a coherent, lethargic, and indifferent state.

Question 6

(a) The author was coherent but largely unmotivated.
(b) The rain undermined Keith's mental state, but he could still think clearly.
(c) He was relaxed and understood by those around him but felt indifferent.
(d) None of the above

Question 7

(a) It was a haphazard, unusually cold summer day in the city.
(b) Keith had a great deal of poise, and kept it cool, despite his state of confusion.
(c) The author was having one of those days when you can't get it together.
(d) He lives in a state of confusion and does not know when it will happen.

Question 8

(a) His friends were playing a practical joke on him.
(b) Keith thought that his friends were swindling him and expected that his day would improve.
(c) Keith's friends never play jokes on him, but they would untangle him.
(d) The author was hoping the day would improve, but he didn't expect it to.

Question 9

  (a) Keith's fortitude was exonerated by a jury of his peers.
  (b) No matter how down you get, if you keep it together, you can come through.
  (c) Being vindicated for your endurance occurs only on rare occasions.
  (d) All of the above

Question 10

  (a) Once Keith got to the studio, he felt better.
  (b) Native's loft studio is a territory independent from the state of New York.
  (c) Exiting the elevator causes one to assert one's self.
  (d) Native's loft studio is in a state other than New York.

Question 11

  (a) There are railway tracks near Native.
  (b) Keith enjoys eating around people who write and produce music.
  (c) The author appreciates being part of something creative.
  (d) He appreciates savoring the talent of excellent tracks.

Question 12

  (a) Keith strode into Native and shook in response to all of the noise there.
  (b) Due to the cacophony in the studio, the author trembled as he went to walk back out.
  (c) Adrienne Hecker's din in Native's loft studio caused Keith to pace his quivering for a second.
  (d) He had more energy and trembled when he heard a high note over the other music in the studio.

Question 13

  (a) The author "kicked himself" for making lousy coffee.
  (b) The author chastised himself for letting the rain undermine his mood.
  (c) He criticized himself for letting the rain outsmart him.
  (d) Keith was irate because he left raindrops in an otherwise empty cabinet.

Question 14

  (a) The kitchen cabinet did not contain any coffee.
  (b) The author compares the kitchen cabinet to the Sahara Desert.
  (c) The kitchen cabinet is sterile.
  (d) The author went back downstairs to purchase some coffee.

WIDE OPEN SPACES

Listening Exercise

Listen to "Wide Open Spaces" all the way through at least once. Then listen to the song again, and graffiti up the wall with any new or unfamiliar words that you hear. Don't worry if you don't fill up the whole wall . . . but it's plausible that you will!

WIDE OPEN SPACES | Nina Zeitlin | Lyrics by Nina Zeitlin & Mike Pandolfo | Music Written by Nina Zeitlin & Mike Pandolfo | Vocals: Nina Zeitlin | Backing Vocals: Vera Pandolfo | Guitar & Bass Guitar: Joe Mendoza | Produced by Mike Pandolfo

LYRICS

| I used to love you | I thought you were the NEMESIS of all that is bad | (And) you were ENAMORED with me | But now you've changed and we will never (again) have what we (once) had | So I opened my heart to you | Now I open my mind to the freeway | Wide open spaces in view | Still a photo of you on the dashboard baby | You can't ABSTAIN from your OBNOXIOUSNESS | Like a PLAGUE that's OBTUSE and OBSCURE | And you can't REFRAIN from your PREDILECTION | To make me GRAVE and FLAGGING and DEMURE | I hope you RECONCILE your VOLATILE behavior | It's like some CONTAGION, an AFFLICTION getting worse | You're a FLOUNDERING mess, filled with SUPERFLUOUS distress | I feel NOSTALGIC for the man I knew at first | It's OMINOUS and PERNICIOUS to be where I am | (And I) Guess people do change in the end | Every minute with you had felt EFFERVESCENT | Your CONJURATION was a FALLACY, it was all pretend | You left a FISSURE in my heart, and just a FILAMENT of my soul | I never thought (that) I could live without you | I put my CREDENCE in you, MANIFESTING hate in me | It's PLAUSIBLE that we could see this (or anything) through | I am strong, with more VALOR than you | I've gained LUCIDITY | After what you put me through | Now I am strong, but you will never know | 'Cause I am gone and it was you that I had to FORGO

dic•tion•ar•y

Abstain (v)—refrain, desist; give up; do without. Antonym: indulge (v).
The congressmen abstained from voting on a bill that they did not support.
Affliction (n)—illness; cause of suffering; burden.
With an affliction such as arthritis, she found it difficult to walk.

Conjuration (n)—witchcraft; the practice of raising or evoking spirits, demons and storms by rituals or incantations.
Absorbed in conjuration, the witch chanted an incantation over the boiling cauldron.
Contagion (n)—a source of infection or corruption.
The biohazard team successfully contained the contagion.
Credence (n)—credibility, weight, acceptance, belief.
I don't place much credence in what most politicians have to say.
Demure (adj)—reserved, decorous, modest; straight-laced. Antonym: flagrant (adj).
This season many retailers are offering more demure styles in order to quell criticism that their clothing lines have been too licentious.
Effervescent (adj)—1. bubbly, fizzy, sparkling. Antonym: flat (adj).
Soda and other carbonated beverages are effervescent.
Effervescent (adj)—2. lively, vibrant, vivacious. Antonym: withdrawn (adj).
Effervescent and personable, she made new friends easily.
Enamored (v)—smitten; in love with; also idiomatically used in reference to appreciation for an object. Antonym: repelled (v).
She was enamored with the dress and bought it immediately.
Fallacy (n)—myth, lie, falsehood; misguided belief.
Following the disaster in Chernobyl, many people came to believe that "safe nuclear power" is a fallacy.
Filament (n)—fiber, thread, strand.
To generate light, an incandescent bulb passes electricity through a wire filament that glows in response to its electrical resistance.
Fissure (n)—crevice, gap, split, fracture.
In May 2003, "The Old Man of the Mountain," a prominent rock feature on the shoulder of New Hampshire's Profile Mountain, succumbed to fissures that caused it to collapse.
Flagging (adj)—waning, declining, failing, wilting, fading.
The color of my old jersey is flagging after being washed so many times.
Flounder (adj)—struggle, falter; to succumb to difficulty. Antonym: thrive (adj).
The business had been floundering, but the employees and management banded together to save the company.

Forgo (v)—relinquish, skip; go without. Antonym: partake (v).
The CEO decided to forgo her salary to cut back on expenses and to save cash.

Grave (adj)—1. serious, severe, critical. Antonym: trifling (adj).
He cogitated because making the wrong decision would have grave consequences.

Grave (n)—2. burial plot.
Over the weekend, my family went to the cemetery to visit my grandmother's grave.

Lucidity (n)—clarity, intelligibility; a state of coherence or clear understanding. Antonym: incoherence (n).
Assaying the team's loss, the captain gained lucidity when he realized that his showboating kept them from scoring more points.

Manifesting (v)—bringing about; becoming apparent.
Melting ice fields and rising ocean tides indicate that global warming is manifesting itself most dramatically at the earth's poles.

Nemesis (n)—archenemy, adversary, competitor. Antonym: ally (n).
Baseball fans always look forward to the Red Sox squaring off against their nemesis, the Yankees.

Nostalgic (adj)—homesick, reflective, wistful; describes thinking of or longing for an earlier, "simpler" period of one's life.
While preparing for his SATs, he became nostalgic for third grade, when his biggest problem was deciding what lunchbox he was going to bring to school.

Obnoxious (adj)—exhibiting insufferable, repugnant behavior.
I wonder if reality show producers actually look for self-absorbed, loud, obnoxious idiots to create drama on their programs.

Obscure (adj)—little known. Antonym: common (adj).
Sometimes unsigned, obscure, independent recording artists create the most innovative music.

Obtuse (adj)—1. stupid, thick, dull-witted. Antonym: clever (adj).
It doesn't mean I'm obtuse because I don't understand quantum physics.

Obtuse (adj)—2. angled between 90 and 180 degrees.
An obtuse angle is between 90 and 180 degrees.

Ominous (adj)—foreboding, forbidding, menacing, threatening. Antonym: welcoming (adj).
It was tornado season and we saw ominous, black clouds hanging low on the horizon.

Pernicious (adj)—evil, malicious, harmful. Antonym: nice (adj).
Many parents regard violent video games as a pernicious influence on children.

Plague (n)—1. outbreak, pestilence, scourge, blight.
The Black Plague, which was spread by rat fleas during the 1340s, killed almost one third of the entire population of Europe.

Plague (v)—2. trouble, pester, bother.
I've been plagued by writer's block and I haven't been able to finish this book.

Plausible (adj)—believable, credible, possible, likely. Antonym: unlikely (adj).
As far as scientists can tell, a catastrophic meteor impact is the most plausible cause of the onset of the ice age.

Predilection (n)—liking, partiality, penchant, tendency; disposition toward.
She has a predilection for sneakers and owns more than fifty pairs.

Reconcile (v)—settle, square; make amends.
The players' union and the team owners met to reconcile their differences so the new season could get underway.

Refrain (v)—1. abstain; to avoid doing something. Antonym: indulge (v).
The waiter asked the restaurant patron with the cigar, "Sir, would you please refrain from smoking?"

Refrain (n)—2. chorus; a poetic or musical verse that repeats; idiomatically refers to a repeated excuse.
Politicians' passing the blame has long been a familiar refrain.

Superfluous (adj)—extraneous, unnecessary, excess.
I can't believe how much superfluous technology auto manufacturers build into today's cars—seriously, does anyone really need a seat that massages your backside while you drive?

Valor (n)—bravery, courage, fearlessness.
John Wayne once said, "Valor is being scared to death but saddling up anyway."

Volatile (adj)—unstable, erratic, impulsive, unpredictable. Antonym: stable (adj).
The Middle East is an historically volatile region, and we can only hope that its people will one day know peace.

SYNONYM MATCHI♪G

Match the following words with their synonyms. Note the letter of the matching synonym in the space adjacent to the word.

_____ Abstain

_____ Affliction

_____ Conjuration   _____ Manifest

_____ Contagion   _____ Nemesis

_____ Credence   _____ Nostalgic

_____ Demure   _____ Obnoxious

_____ Effervescent   _____ Obscure

_____ Enamored   _____ Obtuse

_____ Fallacy   _____ Ominous

_____ Filament   _____ Pernicious

_____ Fissure   _____ Plague

_____ Flag   _____ Plausible

_____ Flounder   _____ Predilection

_____ Forgo   _____ Reconcile

_____ Grave   _____ Refrain

_____ Lucidity   _____ Superfluous

     _____ Valor

     _____ Volatile

(a) credible
(b) falsehood
(c) clarity
(d) archenemy
(e) falter
(f) wane
(g) wistful
(h) witchcraft
(i) cause of suffering
(j) apparent
(k) serious
(l) reserved
(m) outbreak
(n) insufferable
(o) evil
(p) avoid doing
(q) thread
(r) source of infection
(s) partiality
(t) relinquish
(u) erratic
(v) settle
(w) extraneous
(x) crevice
(y) bravery
(z) smitten
(a1) fizzy
(a2) stupid
(a3) refrain
(a4) foreboding
(a5) credibility
(a6) vague

sentencecompl@tion

Using a form or tense of the words below, find the one to best complete each of the following sentences.

WORD BANK

Abstain	Fallacy	Manifesting	Plague
Affliction	Filament	Nemesis	Plausible
Conjuration	Fissure	Nostalgic	Predilection
Contagion	Flagging	Obnoxiousness	Reconcile
Credence	Floundering	Obscure	Refrain
Demure	Forgo	Obtuse	Superfluous
Effervescent	Grave	Ominous	Valor
Enamored	Lucidity	Pernicious	Volatile

1. The General bestowed a medal on the private for his _____ in battle.

2. The bird flu virus is a _____ that was thought only to affect chickens and other fowl but now appears to also be harmful to humans.

3. The Department of Homeland security issued an _____ warning to be on the lookout for suspicious activity.

4. She decided to _____ her bonus and instead gave it to charity.

5. He was in _____ condition after the accident.

6. She was always loud, crass, and _____ .

7. He plays the tenor sax and has a _____ for John Coltrane and jazz from the 1950s.

8. It goes without saying that every superhero needs a _____ to battle.

9. "I'd like to believe that your grandmother ate your homework, but couldn't you at least try to give me a _____ explanation?"

10. Surprisingly, human beings' small toes are _____ and do not help us to stand.

11. Some people are just _____ —you can explain something to them a thousand times, but they still don't get it.

12. Although we couldn't stand one another, we sat down face to face and worked to _____ our differences.

13. Around the holidays I become _____ for the Thanksgiving dinners that we used to have at my grandmother's house.

14. The hurricane first _____ as a tropical storm in the south Caribbean.

15. He was practiced in the art of _____ and referred to himself as a *warlock*.

16. Mount St. Helens is a _____ , active volcano located 50 miles northeast of Portland, Oregon.

17. After she dumped him for being obnoxious, he made up _____ , hurtful claims about her.

18. While perusing an _____ journal that was written around 1850, a researcher uncovered new information about Lincoln's hat.

19. Pressure in the volcanic vent decreased after steam was released through a new _____ in the bedrock.

20. Unable to agree on the details of any issue, the peace talks' negotiators are _____ in their effort to reconcile their positions.

21. Research shows that children are drinking coffee, but they should _____ from consuming large quantities of caffeine until after the age of 18.

22. In light of the fact that his grandmother likes to eat paper, there might be some _____ to his claim that she ate his homework.

23. Compelled by an anxious electorate and no employment growth, the candidates have focused on the _____ job market.

24. The United Nations has asked China to _____ from imprisoning human rights activists.

25. Would-be terrorists are _____ airlines with bomb hoaxes and other disruptions to their operations.

26. According to the Center for Disease Control, noise-induced hearing loss is currently the most common occupational _____ .

27. She recently became _____ with photography and now she never leaves the house without her camera.

28. Unfortunately, seniors often begin to lose their _____ as they become older and the aging process accelerates.

29. Automotive lighting technology has made significant advances over the past few years, discarding incandescent _____ in favor of electro-reactive gases like xenon.

30. When monks first accidentally created champagne in the 1680s, its _____ was an undesirable trait that was regarded as a sign of poor wine making.

31. Their group was reprimanded for spreading _____ , hurtful rumors about other students.

32. Preparing to address the delegates, the keynote speaker adopted a _____ , restrained tone of voice and a formal posture.

SYNONYM SENTENCES

In these sentences, use a form or tense of the words below to match their **bolded** synonyms, and write your choice in the space provided following each sentence.

Abstain	Fallacy	Manifesting	Plague
Affliction	Filament	Nemesis	Plausible
Conjuration	Fissure	Nostalgic	Predilection
Contagion	Flagging	Obnoxiousness	Reconcile
Credence	Floundering	Obscure	Refrain
Demure	Forgo	Obtuse	Superfluous
Effervescent	Grave	Ominous	Valor
Enamored	Lucidity	Pernicious	Volatile

WORD BANK

1. I wish that she would **refrain** from blowing her nose into her shirt because she's grossing me out. _____

2. There isn't a **strand** of truth to his claim that he's the queen's son. _____

3. He had a difficult time responding to his opponent's arguments and **struggled** throughout the debate. _____

4. Dr. Evil is Austin Power's **archenemy**. _____

5. Given the fact that there are an infinite number of galaxies, it is entirely **possible** that there is intelligent life somewhere in the universe. _____

6. The band's tour was canceled due to **waning** ticket sales. _____

7. She's a pathological liar and I don't put an ounce of **belief** in anything she has to say. _____

8. Don't you hate when you can't get a song's **chorus** out of your head even though you haven't heard it in three days? _____

9. My parents love my current girlfriend, but I think that she's too **reserved** for my liking. _____

10. Recording her expenses when they occur makes it is easier for her to **square** her checkbook with her bank statement. _____

11. The **source of infection** was traced to a research lab that was active during the cold war. _____

12. The event's **vivacious** host welcomed everyone personally. _____

13. The prevalence of brutality and bloodshed on TV has the **harmful** effect of desensitizing people to violence. _____

14. Despite its complexities, she described the process with great **clarity**, which gave us a better understanding of how it would progress. _____

15. It is interesting that even the brightest people will believe almost any **falsehood** if it is repeated frequently enough. _____

16. Predicated upon **raising spirits**, Vodun (also known as *Voodoo*) is a religion that has been practiced in West Africa for more than 6,000 years. _____

17. Since we don't have the data yet, we'll **skip** meeting until next week. _____

18. An alien variety of seaweed is posing a **serious** threat to the indigenous species of the Mediterranean's sea bed. _____

19. Recent leading financial indicators have been extremely **unpredictable**, underscoring the uncertain state of the economy. _____

20. I thought that I had made my point clearly, but it seems that he was too **thick** to grasp it. _____

21. Her fiancé is totally **insufferable**; the first time he came over he headed straight for the fridge and then whined that we didn't have any cheese. _____

22. She's been **troubled** by self-doubt and just can't seem to shake it. _____

23. The **illness** is weakening his immune system, making him more susceptible to infection. _____

24. Due to the city's budget woes, a new round of service cuts and tax increases are **becoming apparent.** _____

25. Unencumbered by **unnecessary** posturing, her performance was raw and inspiring. _____

26. Away at college, he was swept up by a wave of **homesickness** and decided to call some old friends. _____

27. Although the score was tied, they won the match due to an old, **little-known** technicality. _____

28. They're so **smitten** with one another that the entire world around them could crumble and they would barely notice. _____

29. With an equal number of classes in favor of and against the proposed changes, a **split** in the student body was exposed. _____

30. A fearless warrior, Joan of Arc was renowned for her faith and **courage.** _____

31. Given the growing deficit and declining tax income, the budget situation appears **threatening.** _____

32. Considering her **penchant** for yellow, I was surprised that she bought a blue car. _____

THE ARTICLE

Read the following article and then, for each question, select the one statement that best describes the author's remarks.

NINA ZEITLIN LONGS FOR "WIDE OPEN SPACES"

NYC—It is plausible that I've stumbled upon an ominous trend manifesting itself in Nina Zeitlin's work. Perhaps afflicted by some contagion, Nina can't seem to abstain from her predilection for writing nostalgic songs about her nemesis... pernicious men. Now I'm plagued by my efforts to reconcile the volatility of her grade subject matter with the effervescent, and occasionally demure, Nina we know and love.

Perhaps she's enamored with guys who are simply wrong for her, but she can't refrain from dating obnoxious, obtuse jerks because she's bolstered by valor. They then conjure a seductive web, but it is only a matter of time until fissures appear in their relationship, their mutual attractions flag, and they begin to flounder.

This may be a fallacy, and I don't put a lot of credence in my superfluous conjecturing, but it is always possible that I've found an obscure filament of truth. Then again, maybe I'm flirting with lucidity and I should forgo playing shrink.—*Keith London*

Question 1

(a) It is possible that the author is clumsy and has fallen on a treadmill.

(b) The author thinks that he may have fallen into a trap that was set in Nina's work.

(c) The author believes that he may have found a foreboding trend in Nina's songs.

(d) It is plausible that the author has identified a singular trend in Nina's songs.

Question 2

(a) Nina has fallen ill and she cannot refrain from waxing nostalgic.

(b) Nina cannot desist from writing songs about being homesick.

(c) Nina can't give up writing songs about simpler times and evil men.

(d) Nina seems disposed to writing reflective songs about her bad relationships.

Question 3

(a) Nina wants to be a superhero whose archenemies are evil men.

(b) She writes songs about relationships with men who aren't good for her.

(c) Nina's adversaries are malicious men.

(d) She enjoys crime-fighting male villains in her spare time.

Question 4

(a) The author cannot square his image of Nina with her heated lyrics.

(b) Keith's attempts to settle Nina's instability have been troubling.

(c) The author is looking to settle his difficulties with Nina.

(d) Keith is concerned that Nina's erratic behavior might be serious.

Question 5

(a) The subject matter of Nina's songs may be considered grave because she is describing men who are erratic.

(b) The subject matter of Nina's songs may be considered volatile because she is describing men who are pernicious.

(c) The subject matter of Nina's songs may be considered grave because she is describing men who are volatile.

(d) The subject matter of Nina's songs may be considered volatile because she is describing men who are erratic.

Question 6

(a) The author is concerned that Nina is unstable; sometimes she's serious, sometimes she's bubbly, and at other times she is reserved.

(b) Nina's vibrant and sometimes decorous; her personality belies the resentment captured by her lyrics.

(c) Nina's fizzy, modest, personality belies the volatility captured by her lyrics.

(d) None of the above

Question 7

(a) It is possible that she is smitten with guys who are wrong for her, but she can't keep herself from dating loutish, stupid idiots.

(b) Perhaps Nina appreciates guys who are wrong for her, but she can't recite the chorus of songs to them because they're thick.

(c) The author conjectures that it is plausible that Nina falls for jerks because she always has an excuse.

(d) Nina is unable to avoid dating dull-witted repugnant louts because she appreciates them for who they are.

Question 8

(a) Nina is courageous to date stupid jerks.

(b) Keith suggests that Nina fearlessly dates louts.

(c) The author poses that Nina's courage encourages her to date jerks.

(d) Nina's valor caused her to start a new extreme sport, "Jerk Dating."

Question 9

(a) Nina's ex-boyfriends put on a good face at first, then, once they're dating, problems arise as they begin to reveal their true nature.

(b) The author conjectures that Nina's ex-boyfriends practice witchcraft and cast spells that split relationships.

(c) The author posits that Nina's jerk ex-boyfriends use incantations to ensnare her but their enchantments flag over time.

(d) Nina's evil, jerk ex-boyfriend is Spiderman.

Question 10

(a) Her ex-boyfriends offer her the gift of a flag dedicated to her.

(b) Their appreciation for one another wilts and they begin to thrash.

(c) Their attraction to one another wanes and their relationship begins to struggle.

(d) To save their relationship, the boyfriends take her to Six Flags.

Question 11

(a) The author proposes that he is lying and doesn't believe himself.

(b) Keith suggests that his inferences may be a misguided belief and he doesn't put much weight in his theories.

(c) Keith suggests that his inferences stem from a misguided belief of unquestionable credibility.

(d) The article's supposition is a myth that he doesn't regard as acceptable.

Question 12

(a) He may have found a little-known thread of truth in his unnecessary lecturing.
(b) The author feels that his extra conjecturing may be a little-known thread.
(c) The author's extraneous positing may have found a vague strand.
(d) Keith regards his analysis of Nina's work as extraneous, but he also says that there may be some truth to his inferences.

Question 13

(a) Keith is flirting with a young woman named Lucidity and should stop.
(b) The author is not a licensed professional trained to deal with issues of lucidity.
(c) The author questions his sanity and says that he should stop overanalyzing things.
(d) The author is nuts and he should stop pretending to be Sigmund Freud.

Wait a minute—my vocab IS **effervescent**!

HOT

SYNONYM MATCHING

(l)	Conflagration	fire		(m)	Profusion	excess
(y)	Decree	declaration		(b)	Propagate	spread
(a2)	Devoid	lacking		(a8)	Proximity	nearness
(a1)	Exhilarating	thrilling		(i)	Pursue	follow
(s)	Fluctuation	variation		(z)	Raze	level
(q)	Follicles	holes in skin		(p)	Rectify	correct
(d)	Frigid	cold		(a9)	Remedy	cure
(a4)	Frustrating	annoying		(k)	Saturate	soak
(t)	Fusion	join		(r)	Seclusion	isolation
(g)	Ignite	kindle		(o)	Sedentary	inactive
(v)	Illusion	delusion		(j)	Stimulate	inspire
(u)	Indefatigable	unrelenting		(a)	Tundra	arctic plain
(a5)	indisputable	certain		(e)	Ungainly	awkward
(x)	Invigorating	revitalizing		(c)	Uniformity	standardization
(a3)	Marquee	canopy		(a7)	Union	combination
(h)	Monotony	repetitiveness		(w)	Vacillation	indecision
(f)	Perpetuate	continue		(n)	Waver	hesitate
(a6)	Peruse	scrutinize				

sentence completion

1. During the debate, his opponent found his remarks to be **indisputable**, making it difficult for him to debate against him.

2. He is following his dream by **pursuing** a career in law.

3. An open, rolling plain, there is little vegetation on the **tundra**.

4. Her **follicles** were damaged over the years by the constant dying and straightening of her hair.

5. The **conflagration** that razed the forest is thought to have been started by a cigarette.

6. The presidential candidates are **propagating** their ideas by making speeches throughout the country.

7. She was **frustrated** by her little brother's refusal to move his feet off of her books.

8. My backpack was **ungainly** because it had too many books in it.

9. The Olympic torch was **ignited** during the opening ceremony in Athens.

10. The **decree** declared that the country would be handed over to its new government.

11. She enjoys the college classes that she's taking, and she finds them very **stimulating**.

12. Her income is never steady; it usually **fluctuates** between $40,000 and $100,000 a year.

13. It's as though he's an immovable, **sedentary** blob; he's always vegging out in front of the television.

14. We have to get that boy out of the house; he'd find my new morning exercise program **invigorating**.

15. The numbing **monotony** of her life bored her, eventually leading her to quit her job to travel around the world.

16. Working to figure out what was wrong, the technicians were doing everything they could to **rectify** the problem.

17. My grandmother believes that the best **remedy** for a cold is homemade chicken soup.

18. His plan to ride a ferret across the country defies logic and is **devoid** of any sense.

19. She is an **indefatigable** competitor who gives 100 percent of herself during every game.

20. In some cultures women are kept in **seclusion** and are rarely seen in public.

21. While I'm editing the book, I need to **peruse** the exercises to verify that everything makes sense.

22. Alaska isn't always **frigid**; as a matter of fact, during the summer it can get quite hot.

23. The building's manager decided to replace the **marquee** over the main entrance.

24. The best thing about the location of my office is its **proximity** to my house.

25. The studio released its latest movie and inundated the press with a **profusion** of PR materials.

26. I've heard that hang gliding is **exhilarating** and that there is no thrill that can compare.

27. At the end of the day, I'm tired and my concentration tends to **waver**.

28. His music is described as a **fusion** of hip hop and alternative styles.

29. The novel *1984* is a cautionary tale that describes the monotony of a society based on **uniformity**.

30. The aim of the preservation society is to **perpetuate** the cultures and traditions of their country.

31. She is **vacillating** between taking a job that is closer to home and a job that offers more money.

32. The next door neighbors **razed** their house and are building an entirely new one on the same foundation.

33. The massive corporate merger is reported to be a **union** of equals.

34. Mirages are only **illusions** caused by the heat rising off of the desert sand, which distorts the view of the horizon.

35. The tie-dying instructions require you to **saturate** the shirt with water before you place it in the dye.

SYNONYM SENTENCES

1. Stock prices **fluctuate** day to day.

2. During the long winters the **tundra** is barren and cold.

3. The **conflagration** spread quickly, but, thankfully, no one was hurt.

4. I enjoy reading the newspaper because I find it **stimulating**.

5. Her mother always said, "**Pursue** your dreams."

6. He **ignited** the campfire with a match.

7. We will do whatever is necessary to **rectify** the situation.

8. The researcher **perused** the results of the study prior to making any announcements regarding its outcome.

9. She was an **indefatigable** protester against animal testing and didn't end her boycott until the company agreed to release its monkeys.

10. When he does his homework, he likes to **seclude** himself.

11. She had made her dream come true; her name was in lights on the theater **marquee**.

12. It isn't always easy making choices and sometimes I **vacillate**.

13. I'm not sure that those dance lessons are helping him out very much; he still looks **ungainly** when he does his routine.

14. I find it **frustrating** when people jostle me to get into the subway.

15. This summer she has a job in a factory, putting popsicle sticks in molds all day, and she said that the **monotony** is going to drive her crazy.

16. As a result of his **sedentary** lifestyle, he was 50 pounds overweight.

17. A native of southern California, he finds Massachusetts **frigid**.

18. The best **remedy** for the flu is to drink lots of fluids and get some rest.

19. He **wavered** before asking her out on a date.

20. The community group was the result of a **union** of different factions from throughout the area.

21. When manufacturing consumer goods, it is important to have a measure of **uniformity** to ensure that each item produced is the same.

22. Despite the **profusion** of TV channels, I can never find anything to watch.

23. My dad says, "Of course you can't find anything good on, TV is **devoid** of anything intellectually stimulating."

24. Our parents bought our house based on its **proximity** to a good school.

25. He was traumatized at the circus when he was a kid, so he now lives in **perpetual** fear of little dogs riding bicycles.

26. After the hurricane severely damaged the house, we needed to **raze** it and build a new one.

27. The defendant's lawyer stated, "Given the facts of the case, it is **indisputable** that my client is innocent."

28. The special-interest group worked to **propagate** rumors about the competing candidate.

29. The sponge won't hold any more liquid—it's **saturated**.

30. We went to an interesting restaurant last night where the cuisine was a **fusion** of Cuban and Chinese foods.

31. Four-foot-three inches tall and 90 pounds, he had no **illusions** that he was going to win a round against the boxing champ.

32. My visit to the day spa was **invigorating**.

33. My friend said that bungee jumping in New Zealand was **exhilarating**, although I'm not sure that I'd want to try it.

34. The crazy king issued a **decree** stating that all of the country's citizens were required to wear their socks on the outside of their shoes.

35. If you look closely at your arm, you can see the **follicles** in your skin.

THE ARTICLE

1. (b) The author enjoys working with Rodney and Keith.

2. (c) The author is using fire as a metaphor to describe the intensity of the artists' music.

3. (a) The artists combine different musical styles to create a unique sound.

4. (a) Avon is a tireless and inspiring performer.

5. (d) Avon Marshall is a genuinely gifted performer and is very comfortable in the studio.

6. (b) Keith and Rodney write music that mixes it up.

7. (a) The artists' music forges its own path, breaking the typical boundaries present in today's play lists.

8. (d) The author finds the artists' music energizing and regards it as a metaphorical cure for one's state of well-being.

9. (b) The artists are making it in the music industry and are building their reputations.

10. (a) The author expects the artists to perform publicly, sell their CDs in stores, and become famous.

11. (c) The artists and author have worked closely, giving the author an appreciation for the artists' combination of talents and their preparedness for stardom.

12. (b) Rodney and Keith are working hard to achieve stardom.

Acquiesce Amorous Aroma Awkward Consummate
Conversely Deleterious Delirium Ecstasy Enamored Futile
Incantation Inevitably Infatuation Inimitable Interminable
Intuit Laborious Prosimity Reticence Senescent Shroud
Situation Synchronously Tortuous Tranquility Acquiesce
Amorous Aroma Awkward Consummate Conversely
Deleterious Delirium Ecstasy Enamored Futile Incantation
Inevitably Infatuation Inimitable Interminable Intuit Laborious
Prosimity Reticence Senescent Shroud Situation
Synchronously Tortuous Tranquility Acquiesce Amorous
Aroma Awkward Consummate Conversely Deleterious
Delirium Ecstasy Enamored Futile Incantation Inevitably
Infatuation Inimitable Interminable Intuit Laborious Prosimity
Reticence Senescent Shroud Situation Synchronously
Tortuous Tranquility Acquiesce Amorous Aroma Awkward
Consummate Conversely Deleterious Delirium Ecstasy
Enamored Futile Incantation Inevitably Infatuation Inimitable
Interminable Intuit Laborious Reticence Senescent
Shroud Situation Synchronously Tortuous Tranquility
Acquiesce Amorous Aroma Awkward Consummate
Conversely Deleterious Delirium Ecstasy Enamored Futile
Incantation Inevitably Infatuation Inimitable Interminable
Intuit Laborious Reticence Senescent Shroud
Situation Synchronously Tortuous Tranquility Acquiesce
Amorous Aroma Awkward Consummate Conversely
Deleterious Delirium Ecstasy Enamored Futile Incantation
Inevitably Infatuation Inimitable Interminable Intuit Laborious
Prosimity Reticence Senescent Shroud Situation
Synchronously Tortuous Tranquility Acquiesce Amorous
Aroma Awkward Consummate Conversely Deleterious
Delirium Ecstasy Enamored Futile Incantation Inevitably
Infatuation Inimitable Interminable Intuit Laborious Prosimity
Reticence Senescent Shroud Situation Synchronously
Tortuous Tranquility Acquiesce Amorous Aroma Awkward
Consummate Conversely Deleterious Delirium Ecstasy
Enamored Futile Incantation Inevitably Infatuation Inimitable

The Good and Honorable Reverend Gil, working the soundboard

ALREADY TAKEN

SYNONYM MATCHING

(g)	Acquiesce	agree	(s)	Infatuation	fixation
(u)	Amorous	affectionate	(t)	Inimitable	unique
(k)	Aroma	pleasing scent	(c)	Interminable	endless
(r)	Awkward	uncomfortable	(i)	Intuit	perceive
(n)	Consummate	archetypal	(v)	Laboriously	gruelingly
(e)	Conversely	contrary	(l)	Proximity	nearness
(y)	Deleterious	harmful	(w)	Reticence	reluctance
(z)	Delirium	disorientation	(q)	Senescent	aging
(j)	Ecstasy	joy	(m)	Shrouded	covered
(o)	Enamored	smitten	(h)	Situation	predicament
(x)	Futile	useless	(f)	Synchronously	simultaneous
(b)	Incantation	spell	(a)	Tortuous	arduous
(d)	Inevitably	certainly	(p)	Tranquility	peacefulness

sentence completion

1. We live in close **proximity** to our neighbors.

2. Time never stops and **inevitably**, everything changes.

3. She was in a state of **ecstasy** when she was accepted to Yale.

4. In the United States people drive on the right-hand side of the road; **conversely**, in Britain, you would drive on the left-hand side.

5. The hikers' route through the mountain pass was **tortuous**.

6. When the boxer regained consciousness after getting knocked out, he awoke in a state of **delirium**.

7. The president of the student government **acquiesced** to the demands of the student body.

8. Professionals working in the fashion industry strive to create their own **inimitable** style.

9. His father's stories about his childhood were **interminable**.

10. Given the fact that she can't sing, it's **futile** for her to try out for *American Idol* unless she wants to be on the blooper episode!

11. The hood of the explorer's parka **shrouded** her face.

12. My mother became **enamored** with my father the first time she saw him.

13. I love the **tranquility** of the ocean when the weather is calm.

14. She could **intuit** that I was worried about my upcoming exam.

15. Feeding a dog chocolate can be **deleterious** to its health.

16. She was **infatuated** with her favorite band, and she listened to their CD constantly.

17. The **aroma** of freshly baked pastries filled the air.

18. She created an awkward **situation** by asking me to help her cheat on the test.

19. It was **awkward** for me to see my dad dating after my parents got divorced.

20. The witches chanted an **incantation** around a boiling potion.

21. A **consummate** professional, she managed the meeting flawlessly.

22. After the banquet, he **laboriously** washed every dish by hand.

23. She was **reticent** to speak in front of the class.

24. On some SUVs the front wheels move **synchronously** with the back wheels.

25. The 14-year-old cat is **senescent**.

26. The two lovers gazed at one another **amorously**.

SYNONYM SENTENCES

1. The bakery was filled with the **aroma** of fresh bread.

2. If you don't have a CD player, it's **futile** to try to listen to a CD.

3. She discovered an **amorous** love letter in her locker.

4. The sorceress' **incantation** made him fall in love with a chicken.

5. Her style is **inimitable**.

6. The **situation** she found herself in was unsettling.

7. When two things occur at the same time, they happen **synchronously**.

8. She was **ecstatic** when she found out that she had won the Nobel Prize.

9. Although she didn't tell him, he could **intuit** when she was mad at him.

10. Although my workout is only an hour long, it seems **interminable**.

11. I am **infatuated** with romantic novels.

12. He **acquiesced** to their demands.

13. I am not **enamored** with BMW's new designs.

14. Polished and poised, she was the **consummate** professional.

15. They were the consummate odd couple; she was outgoing, and **conversely**, he was shy.

16. The bus was in such **proximity** to my car that it almost hit us.

17. After the accident, the driver was in a state of **delirium**.

18. When going on a first date I always feel **awkward**.

19. Shaking a baby can be **deleterious** to the child's health.

20. I enjoy the **tranquility** of a quiet afternoon.

21. It is **inevitable** that children will grow up.

22. The old crumbling building is **senescent**.

23. He was **reticent** to share his opinions with the class.

24. Often the path to success is **tortuous**.

25. The first snowfall of winter **shrouded** the hills.

26. Writing a novel by hand is a **laborious** task.

ARTICLE

1. (c) After many requests, Mia agreed to do the interview with resignation.

2. (b) Recording a full-length CD is grueling work.

3. (d) Mia has her own unique style.

4. (d) Mia sings about the difficulty of falling for someone who cannot reciprocate.

5. (b) She acknowledges that she can't date her best friend's boyfriend.

6. (c) Her predicament has left her feeling uncomfortable

7. (a) She did not readily discuss about whom she may have written the song.

8. (c) "Already Taken" uses music to give the listener contrasting feelings.

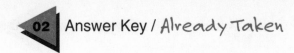

9. (a) "Already Taken" is like a mystical chant that causes the listener to remember.

10. (d) Mia is obsessed with her girlfriend's boyfriend and the situation is awkward.

11. (a) The boyfriend secretly likes her but can't break up with her friend.

12. (b) Mia's storytelling reflects vitality rather than sadness.

SHINE

SYNONYM MATCHING

(o)	Actuate	motivate		(n)	Rabid	fanatical
(m)	Captivated	charmed		(i)	Renovate	refurbish
(b)	Dregs	sediment		(f)	Resplendent	dazzling
(a)	Forsake	abandon		(q)	Scoff	mock
(l)	Illuminate	clarify		(d)	Seclusion	isolation
(p)	Incite	goad		(j)	Skulk	sneak
(e)	Lurk	lie-in-wait		(c)	Solace	comfort
(r)	Martyred	subjugated		(g)	Vacillation	indecision
(h)	Mired	caught up		(k)	Welter	confusion

sentence completion

1. Her children gave her **solace** after her husband's death.

2. The demonstrator was overrun by government forces and died a **martyr** for his cause.

3. Paparazzi often **lurk** in the bushes around celebrities' homes, waiting to ambush them.

4. He was so embarrassed after pouring a drink down the front of his pants that he **skulked** away from the party.

5. She was bitten by a hamster when she was a child, and she's had a **rabid** hatred of them ever since.

6. Critics **scoffed** at Henry Ford's early attempts to build a car.

7. He was fired for **inciting** co-workers to rebel against the new company rules.

8. The story and the beauty of the film **captivated** audiences around the world.

9. She **vacillated** between going to Florida and going to California.

10. The entire building was **renovated** after asbestos was found in the walls.

11. Their strong commitment to their community **actuated** them to volunteer.

12. Despite our differences, I would never **forsake** my family.

13. The queen wore a **resplendent** jewel-encrusted gown.

14. Seeking **seclusion**, the reclusive star flew to a private island.

15. There was a **welter** of CDs and cassettes to look through at the garage sale.

16. The diary she left behind **illuminated** her thinking and clarified why she ran off with the guy who runs the deli.

17. As the horse pulled the wagon, its wheels became **mired** in the mud.

18. She drank the chocolate milk down to the **dregs**.

SYNONYM SENTENCES

1. He decided to **renovate** the house.

2. Her diamond earrings were **resplendent**.

3. He **vacillated** between having smooth or chunky peanut butter.

4. His blue eyes **captivated** the girls.

5. The girls **scoffed at** his attempt to join the field hockey team.

6. The professor **illuminated** the themes conveyed in Shakespeare's plays.

7. The prisoner was placed in **seclusion** after disobeying the warden.

8. I found the cat **lurking** in the bushes, stalking the birds.

9. In an effort to **actuate** the players, the coach gave an impassioned speech at halftime.

10. She found **solace** in her friends after losing her job.

11. I've been **mired** in work at the studio.

12. The escaped convict was found **skulking** around the city.

13. The professor's office was a **welter** of books, papers, and scientific bric-a-brac.

14. We arrived late to the sale, and the earlier shoppers only left behind the **dregs** of what the store had to offer.

15. She is a **rabid** basketball fan.

16. He was **inciting** the crowd to riot.

17. Would you **forsake** your beliefs for money?

18. He went to prison for speaking his mind about the government and **martyred** himself for his beliefs.

ARTICLE

1. (b) His performances have enthralled audiences.
2. (c) "Shine" is the product of Joe's individual creativity.
3. (d) The song "Shine" is a glorious, brilliant declaration.
4. (a) The career path he chose was not traditional.
5. (c) His path unclear, he struggled with the confusion of youth.
6. (a) Joe moved between jobs while he was finding himself.
7. (d) During his period of indecision, he wasn't suffering.
8. (a) Joe did not want to fanatically chase fame and fortune.
9. (b) Joe was a great mechanic who worked on Porsches.
10. (d) His motivation was his love of music, and Todd showed him the way.
11. (c) He didn't seek the limelight, but he was comfortable there.
12. (d) None of the above

Acquiesce Amorous Aroma Awkward Consummate
Conversely Deleterious Delirium Ecstasy Enamored Futile
Incantation Inevitably Infatuation Inimitable Interminable
Intuit Laborious Prosimity Reticence Senescent Shroud
Situation Synchronously Tortuous Tranquility Acquiesce
Amorous Aroma Awkward Consummate Conversely
Deleterious Delirium Ecstasy Enamored Futile Incantation
Inevitably Infatuation Inimitable Interminable Intuit Laborious
Prosimity Reticence Senescent Shroud Situation
Synchronously Tortuous Tranquility Acquiesce Amorous
Aroma Awkward Consummate Conversely Deleterious
Delirium Ecstasy Enamored Futile Incantation Inevitably
Infatuation Inimitable Interminable Intuit Laborious Prosimity
Reticence Senescent Shroud Situation Synchronously
Tortuous Tranquility Acquiesce Amorous Aroma Awkward
Consummate Conversely Deleterious Delirium Ecstasy
Enamored Futile Incantation Inevitably Infatuation Inimitable
Interminable Intuit Laborious Prosimity Reticence Senescent
Shroud Situation Synchronously Tortuous Tranquility
Acquiesce Amorous Aroma Awkward Consummate
Conversely Deleterious Delirium Ecstasy Enamored Futile
Incantation Inevitably Infatuation Inimitable Interminable
Intuit Laborious Prosimity Reticence Senescent Shroud
Situation Synchronously Tortuous Tranquility Acquiesce
Amorous Aroma Awkward Consummate Conversely
Deleterious Delirium Ecstasy Enamored Futile Incantation
Inevitably Infatuation Inimitable Intuit Laborious Prosimity
Reticence Senescent Shroud Situation Synchronously
Tortuous Tranquility Acquiesce Amorous Aroma Awkward
Consummate Conversely Deleterious Delirium Ecstasy
Enamored Futile Incantation Inevitably Infatuation Inimitable

Keith Middleton

WHY DIDN'T YOU TELL ME

SYNONYM MATCHING

(e)	Addiction	dependence	(b)	Decoy	lure
(i)	Affliction	illness	(g)	Entice	persuade
(a)	Alluring	appealing	(k)	Flagrant	blatant
(m)	Assay	evaluate	(t)	Irate	angry
(j)	Cognizant	aware	(v)	Obsession	fixation
(x)	Collaborate	cooperate	(c)	Predisposition	propensity
(q)	Comely	attractive	(r)	Profound	deep
(n)	Complicit	complacent	(p)	Revelation	disclosure
(f)	Conjecture	opine	(s)	Sensual	pleasing
(o)	Conviction	belief	(l)	Sinister	evil
(u)	Crass	rude	(w)	Stolid	dull
(h)	Craven	cowardly	(d)	Surmise	deduce

sentence completion

1. The beautiful Corvette was a **decoy** to lure customers into the used-car lot.

2. Her argument with the store manager caused the woman to become **irate**.

3. The owner tried to **entice** the star player to join the team by offering him a large salary.

4. Looking to incite the players on the home team, the runner said something **crass** about the first baseman's wife.

5. In an earlier era, it was common for people to refer to an attractive woman as being **comely**.

6. The insurance adjuster was very **stolid** and serious about her work.

7. Stalkers are **obsessed** with the celebrities they follow.

8. It is my personal **conviction** that Tibet should be free.

9. Sensual and captivating, her perfume was very **alluring**.

10. Initially, she couldn't figure out how to answer the question, but then she had a **revelation** and solved it right away.

11. She is **addicted** to cigarettes; she wants to smoke all the time.

12. Given the clues, the police **surmised** who was responsible for the robbery.

13. Lack of shelter is one of the many **afflictions** of the homeless.

14. Movie villains are always hatching some **sinister** plot to take over the world.

15. He always gives in because he's **predisposed** to trying to make others happy.

16. The United States is hoping more countries will **collaborate** to rebuild Iraq.

17. The lab needed to **assay** the water for pollutants.

18. The defense had suppressed some evidence, so the jury was not **cognizant** of the full facts of the case.

19. The player was thrown out of the game because of the **flagrant** foul he committed.

20. Eating chocolate is a **sensual** pleasure.

21. There has been a lot of **conjecture** in the media about who will win the election.

22. Abandoning friends in the face of trouble is a **craven** act.

23. He was fired for his **complicity** in the office scandal.

24. The Greek scholar Socrates is considered one of history's most **profound** thinkers.

SYNONYM SENTENCES

1. Saving yourself when others are in danger is **craven**.

2. The two companies will **collaborate** to make the project work.

3. The appraiser will **assay** the antique's value.

4. It is my **conviction** that all people deserve proper health care.

5. He used his charm to **entice** her to go out with him.

6. She is **predisposed** to getting seasick.

7. Her perfume had an **alluring** scent.

8. Loud and obnoxious, he often makes **crass** remarks.

9. When she saw that she had received a parking ticket, she became **irate**.

10. Unable to control himself, he finally accepted that he was **addicted**.

11. Without sufficient information, we can only **conjecture** what the results will be.

12. The guard who opened the lock for the burglars was **complicit** in the crime.
13. The celebrity's two-day marriage was a **flagrant** attempt to gain publicity.
14. In her day, Jacqueline Kennedy was quite **comely**.
15. She was **cognizant** of the implication of her actions.
16. During the spring, many people are **afflicted** by allergies.
17. He isn't flashy at all; he's just a straightforward, **stolid** kind of guy.
18. Silk is renowned for its supple, smooth, **sensual** texture.
19. Electrical appliances have had a **profound** impact on the way we live.
20. By examining the rings of a tree stump, we can **surmise** how old the tree was when it was cut down.
21. Socks were an **obsession** of his and he had hundreds of pairs in every color, pattern, and size.
22. The shocking **revelation** of criminal acts within the department caused a lot of disruption within the community.
23. In a bait-and-switch scam, an unscrupulous business will try to sell customers an inferior product by using a better product as a **decoy**.
24. In video clips, Osama bin Laden reveals a **sinister** smile when he discusses the attack on the World Trade Center.

The ARTICLE

1. (a) Nina began working with Defined Mind shortly after coming to New York City.
2. (d) Nina didn't know what she was getting into.
3. (b) She was interested in writing in a new idiom.
4. (c) She was inspired to write the song and complete it afterward.
5. (b) To gain her love interest's attention, she contemplates the use of a lure.
6. (a) Nina appreciates her crush's knowing, sly smile and confident demeanor.
7. (d) Editing the song took a great deal of time.
8. (a) Nina believes that she wrote a great song.
9. (c) Nina wrote about a comely, outgoing young man.
10. (b) Sammy exists as a subject in this song to convey unattractive qualities.
11. (d) Nina feels it is easier to remember information from songs.

Joe Pascarell

Go!

SYNONYM MATCHI♪♫G

(l)	Accolades	praise	(k)	Inconsequential	trivial
(m)	Accordingly	consequently	(a6)	Intricate	complicated
(p)	Amateur	layperson	(a1)	Labyrinthine	circuitous
(b2)	Annihilate	destroy	(a9)	Lesser	smaller
(s)	Antithesis	opposite	(a5)	Merits	to deserve
(q)	Assure	guarantee	(z)	Momentous	historic
(d)	Bested	surpassed	(j)	Neophyte	novice
(b)	Borders	on the verge of	(a8)	Paradigm	example
(o)	Complex	intricate	(b1)	Perplex	confuse
(y)	Context	circumstances	(b3)	Procure	acquire
(t)	Credit	recognition	·(i)	Pugilistic	belligerent
(a)	Decipher	decode	(a7)	Punitive	retaliatory
(h)	Distraction	disturbance	(u)	Pusillanimous	timid
(r)	Epitome	essence	(x)	Refraction	change in direction
(a4)	Esoteric	arcane	(v)	Revere	admire
(c)	Expertise	proficiency	(a2)	Significant	meaningful
(f)	Fathom	comprehend	(w)	Vantage	advantage
(n)	Frequency	rate of occurrence	(g)	Vertigo	dizziness
(e)	Frequently	regularly	(a3)	Virtuoso	prodigy

sentencecompl@tion

1. We have an easy time talking to each other because we're on the same **frequency**.

2. Many academic institutions are working to improve the state of education and are seeking a new **paradigm**.

3. He played masterfully and we were treated to a **virtuoso** performance.

4. Complex is the **antithesis** of simple.

5. The study's outcome is encouraging and **merits** further study.

6. The route we took was **labyrinthine**, and there isn't any way we would be able to get back without better directions.

7. It was pretty pathetic that they were **bested** by one of the worst teams in the league.

8. She's worked in the discipline for many years and has accumulated significant **expertise** on that particular subject.

9. The roller coaster was too much for him and he was overcome by **vertigo**.

10. It looked intimidating, but we **assured** him that it was safe.

11. **Complex** is the antithesis of simple.

12. Our team **annihilated** the competition and we finished the season undefeated.

13. The chemistry professor instructed us to behave **accordingly** in the lab because, otherwise, we might blow ourselves to bits.

14. We couldn't **fathom** why he went to school wearing a pink tutu.

15. During their discussion, she convinced him to see the issue from her **vantage** point.

16. Like everyone else, I started out as a **neophyte**, but my expertise grew with training and experience.

17. He gave up his **amateur** ranking and went pro this season.

18. When I brought up the topic, she became **pugilistic**, but her tone softened as she came to understand my perspective.

19. I find flashing online ads very **distracting**; they make it difficult to read a site's content.

20. She works at a think tank in Washington, D.C., and spends her time pondering "buy-side economics" and other **esoteric** subjects.

21. Even after hours of interrogation, he wouldn't **decipher** the secret code for his captors.

22. I'll readily acknowledge that it was originally her idea; I have to give **credit** where it's due.

23. It is always gratifying to receive **accolades** and the respect of your peers.

24. His recent unusual behavior **borders** on insanity.

25. The new data we received was **inconsequential** and did not affect our original findings.

26. Since she didn't have any good options, she was forced to choose between the **lesser** of two evils.

27. He was **perplexed** by the toy's complicated assembly instructions.

28. The Dali Lama is **revered** for his wisdom and spiritual insight.

29. Always ready to come through in the clutch, she **epitomized** grace under pressure.

30. Never **pusillanimous**, he fought for what was right.

31. A diamond sparkles because light is **refracted** as it shines through its facets.

32. We need to **procure** some additional equipment before we embark on our camping trip.

33. To best understand historical events, it is important that we view them in **context**.

34. I'm **frequently** preoccupied and forgetful; if my head weren't attached to my shoulders, I would have already lost it somewhere.

35. Chastising the defendant, the judge awarded the plaintiff $100 million in **punitive** damages.

36. The findings of the study were **significant** and caused us to reconsider our position on the issue.

37. Christening the new ship, the captain said, "I would like to say a few words in honor of this **momentous** occasion."

38. He was perplexed by the toy's **intricate** assembly instructions.

SYNONYM SENTENCES

1. Her reasoning was **labyrinthine**, and I still cannot fathom how she arrived at her conclusions.

2. Even though the theater company is **amateur**, their production of *Death of a Salesman* was excellent.

3. Outgoing and friendly, he is the **antithesis** of his curmudgeonly father.

4. She's in great shape because she exercises **frequently**.

5. The defenders **annihilated** the invading forces as they fought to enter the city.

6. His partner created a **distraction** while he absconded with the paintings.

7. Her physician was concerned about her condition; **accordingly**, he conducted a battery of tests to establish a diagnosis.

8. He said that although he authored the piece, she deserves much of the **credit** for their accomplishment.

9. He was overcome by **vertigo** on the Empire State Building's observation deck.

10. It takes years to learn to read and write in Chinese because the language's characters are so **complex**.

11. Hearing barking on a CD that I was playing, my dog stared at the speaker, **perplexed** as to why she couldn't find the other dogs.

12. She couldn't possibly **fathom** that the dogs' barks were recorded and overdubbed into the song.

13. The engineers selected the design based upon its **merits**.

14. The design was well-regarded and received a variety of **accolades**.

15. She **bested** me in three games out of four.

16. I **assured** him we would arrive to the airport in time to make his flight.

17. In college you have the opportunity to explore **esoteric** subject matter that you wouldn't normally encounter outside of an academic setting.

18. She was **revered** for her longstanding role as the community's spiritual leader and its most determined advocate.

19. Underhanded and **pusillanimous**, he ratted out his cronies to the feds to save his own skin.

20. He considers lobbying to be a **lesser** influence on public policy than it is popularly thought to be.

21. The completion of the Brooklyn Bridge was a **momentous** event that marked the dawn of a new age in engineering.

22. She recently earned another belt in karate, but she's still a **neophyte** and has a lot of work to do to build her expertise.

23. She gave a **virtuoso** performance at Carnegie Hall and received a standing ovation.

24. The issue is far more **intricate** than I had first thought, and I'll need to give it further consideration before I make a decision.

25. While visiting Rome, I asked our guide to translate a shopkeeper's comments because I couldn't **decipher** what he was trying to say.

26. I wouldn't call his contributions trivial, but the weren't very **significant** either.

27. I'm not sure how I will respond to her comments; I imagine it will depend on the **context**.

28. My kid brother's new remote control truck didn't work because the remote-control unit was on a different **frequency**.

29. While the article does bring some new information to light, much of it **borders** on fiction.

30. They couldn't hire her because she did not possess the necessary **expertise**.

31. When she asked him to turn off his cell phone during the performance, he became **pugilistic**.

32. She acquiesced to his requests because they were ultimately to her **vantage**.

33. The rover sustained a jolt when it landed, but any damage was **inconsequential**.

34. Since our neighbors weren't willing to repair the damage they caused, our attorney recommended that we take **punitive** measures.

35. In order to execute the plan in its current form it will be necessary for us to **procure** additional resources.

36. Both light and sound waves experience **refraction** as they pass through different materials.

37. General George S. Patton was the **epitome** of the war-hardened military man.

38. In 1954 Steve Allen created the **paradigm** for the modern talk show.

THE ARTICLE

1. (c) Most people call Rodney "RW," but on *Vocab Rock* he is credited as "Rodney Willie."

2. (b) The author regards Rodney as a verbal genius who can surpass even the toughest competitor.

3. (a) Keith Middleton, who writes the music, is an outstanding professional who deserves his own accolades.

4. (d) "Go!" prompted the author to take inventory of Rodney's skill and to complement him.

5. (b) The author believes that Rodney's primary advantage is his considerable intellect.

6. (c) Rodney's towering verses are the product of great inspiration and make other recording artists look inferior.

7. (a) The author feels that Rodney's work dispels the notion that artists who rap are incapable of authoring intellectually challenging material.

8. (b) Timid novices may be befuddled by the complexity of Rodney's work, but appropriately, those who are knowledgeable admire its significance.

9. (d) Those who do not believe that Rodney's work is brilliant are just jealous.

10. (c) The intricacy of Rodney's lyrics regularly makes the author dizzy.

11. (c) Rodney and the author work together well and disruptions that might otherwise interfere with their progress prove to be insignificant.

SUPERGIRL

SYNONYM MATCHING

(m)	Awesome	awe-inspiring	(z)	Loom	overhang
(o)	Benediction	blessing	(c)	Manifest	show
(j)	Bestow	give	(k)	Minimal	smallest
(q)	Candor	openness	(d)	Mire	marsh
(w)	Cosmos	outer space	(s)	Phoenix	redeemed
(r)	Crucial	essential	(n)	Pithy	concise
(v)	Declaration	statement	(b)	Quixotic	idealistic
(t)	Dispel	dismiss	(e)	Resolve	conviction
(u)	Dissolve	disband	(h)	Seep	leak
(y)	Faction	group	(i)	Slander	defame
(p)	Fathom	understand	(f)	Squander	waste
(a1)	Genius	extraordinary intelligence	(x)	Toxin	poison
			(l)	Traversing	traveling
(a2)	Gracious	polite	(g)	Underlying	primary influence
(a)	Infinite	endless			

sentencecompletion

1. The many **toxins** in the air are said to be the cause for the increase in cases of asthma in children.

2. He sought their approval as though it were a **benediction**.

3. She tried to **fathom** what caused her mom's angry reaction.

4. Using the microwave to cook takes a **minimal** amount of effort.

5. After she was offered a satisfactory, but not perfect, job, her dad told her not to **squander** a good opportunity.

6. Looking at the stars, the universe appears to go on into **infinity**.

7. The revolt for political reform originally **manifested** itself as a series of student protests.

8. They had everything ready for our visit to their summer house and were very **gracious** hosts.

9. To look at the earth while walking on the moon must be an **awesome** sight.

10. The stadium proposal was contested by two **factions**, people who supported its construction and others who were against it.

11. After shuffling their lineup, the last-place team came back like a **phoenix** and went on to win the championship.

12. I could see the tornado **looming** on the horizon, so we left the house to look for a safe place.

13. It is **quixotic** to believe that we can eliminate world hunger.

14. The two of them were **mired** in a longstanding argument.

15. I wish they would just sit down, talk it out, and **resolve** it.

16. The winner voluntarily submitted herself to a physical to **dispel** any allegations that she was using anything to enhance her performance.

17. At the start of the initiation ceremony, the new inductees made a **declaration** of faith to the secret society.

18. Occasionally, I gaze at the night sky and stare into the **cosmos**.

19. Oil **seeped** from the tank, contaminating the surrounding soil.

20. He was always respected for his **candor**, even though sometimes he was too honest.

21. The complexity of Mozart's musical composition is evidence of his **genius**.

22. Following the TV reporter's claim that she was a criminal, she sued him for **slander**.

23. Place the pill on your tongue and let it **dissolve**.

24. The Purple Heart is a medal **bestowed** on soldiers for suffering injuries in combat.

25. She apologized for her **pithy** response to my naive question.

26. It is **crucial** that you follow the medication's directions.

27. Lewis and Clark are famous for **traversing** the Louisiana Territory.

28. She disagreed with him because she thought his **underlying** assumptions were wrong.

SYNONYM SENTENCES

1. I can't **fathom** how she could deceive her best friend.

2. During high tide the harbor is filled with water, but while the tide is out it's a **mire**.

3. A few years ago he was down and out, but he worked hard to get his act together and came back like a **phoenix**.

4. Although she was embarrassed to receive the attention of everyone at the event, she was humble and **graciously** accepted the award.

5. Her aspirations were **quixotic**, but she persevered and succeeded.

6. The cosmos seems to be **infinite** at night.

7. At the engagement party, the bride's father **bestowed** his blessings on the couple.

8. If you want to avoid sunburns, it is **crucial** that you wear suntan lotion at the beach.

9. Architect Frank Gehry's buildings, some of which are constructed with wavy walls and titanium cladding, are regarded as works of pure **genius**.

10. The **minimal** amount of pay you can receive for this position is $6 an hour.

11. The **underlying** reason he doesn't go to the movies is that he's afraid of the dark.

12. Reacting to the negative remarks that their paid spokesman made to the press, the company **dissolved** its relationship with him.

13. The sunrise broke over the horizon like a **benediction** on the new day.

14. Having set countless sales records, the Beatles' success still **looms** throughout the music industry, even though they broke up more than thirty years ago.

15. Speaking about **toxins** that exist in nature, the horticulturist warned us that some wild mushrooms are deadly.

16. They **traversed** the mountain range.

17. Hoping he would forgive her, she **candidly** told her boyfriend that she had dated another guy.

18. The new government was in a state of disarray because competing **factions** were fighting for power.

19. Looking to end the standoff, the union and corporate officers made a concerted effort to **resolve** their differences.

20. The hotel room had an **awesome** view of the city skyline.

21. Genuinely concerned for his estranged sister's welfare, he showed up at the hospital to **dispel** the idea that he didn't care.

22. Whenever I come into large amounts of money, I always seem to **squander** it.

23. At the movie premier, the star made a **pithy** remark in response to an interviewer's question about her personal life.

24. The kids from another clique made **slanderous** comments about my sister.

25. Bankrupt, addicted, and forsaken by her family, she **declared** that she would rebuild her life.

26. The planetarium show made me feel as though I were shooting through the **cosmos**.

27. I cut myself slicing a bagel, and the blood **seeped** through the first bandage I put on.

28. She showed **manifest** relief at not having any more exams for the year.

THE ARTICLE

1. (b) They were there to accomplish some important work.

2. (d) The artists openly discussed the ideas behind "SuperGirl."

3. (c) Lyle and Adrienne's music is brilliantly written.

4. (a) The artists have been working together for only a short time.

5. (b) Lyle and Adrienne create great music despite working together only a short time.

6. (d) "SuperGirl" is a great statement of determination.

7. (c) Originally, the authors' thought only older partnerships could create great work.

8. (b) The message of "SuperGirl" is fitting, given today's harsh sociopolitical climate.

9. (a) Adrienne and Lyle understand that hope for world peace is idealistic.

10. (d) The artists can't understand why people choose to treat each other so poorly.

11. (c) Political parties and world leaders say unflattering things about one another.

12. (a) The artists contemplate a time when people will cooperate and allow peace to flourish.

13. (b) The authors appreciated Adrienne and Lyle's wishes for world peace.

THE LETTER

SYNONYM MATCHING

(i)	Abstain	do without	(a)	Forlorn	dejected
(r)	Cardiologist	heart doctor	(g)	Friction	hostility
(k)	Cogitate	ponder	(e)	Ironic	paradoxical
(o)	Colossal	immense	(d)	Jeopardize	risk
(n)	Debilitated	incapacitated	(t)	Panache	style
(s)	Disdain	despise	(h)	Peers	contemporaries
(m)	Duration	time interval	(b)	Poignant	touching
(u)	Elated	euphoric	(f)	Quell	suppress
(l)	Exacting	challenging	(p)	Refrain	abstain
(v)	Extolled	praise	(q)	Surmise	gather
(c)	Fester	irritate	(j)	Tempestuous	emotional

sentence completion

1. Choosing between going away to school or attending college locally and living at home is a **colossal** decision.

2. "I didn't do it" is a familiar **refrain** of the guilty.

3. Examining the skid marks, the investigator **surmised** that the driver did not start braking early enough to avoid the accident.

4. He didn't want to let the problem with his sister **fester**, so he asked her if they could talk it out.

5. I had a terrible case of the flu and I was completely **debilitated**.

6. Thousands packed the canyon of lower Broadway to **extol** John Glenn upon his return as the first American to orbit the Earth.

7. The dean made an impassioned plea for cooler heads to prevail as she tried to **quell** the student uprising.

8. Those who perished on 9/11 were remembered in a **poignant** tribute at the site of the World Trade Center.

9. Talented but **tempestuous**, he was difficult to work with if things didn't go his way.

10. Isn't it **ironic** that "reality" shows are edited?

11. Rivals on the court, they always had **friction** between them.

12. My dad had a heart attack and now visits the **cardiologist** regularly.

13. Sitting in front of their demolished home, they looked **forlorn** but said that they were happy to have survived the hurricane.

14. Since some students are only comfortable talking about their problems with friends, she started a **peer** counseling program at her school.

15. She's a vegetarian and **abstains** from eating meat.

16. He was **elated** by his daughter's safe return from her trek through the Himalayas.

17. The art teacher asked his students to draw cartoons for the **duration** of the class and to bring in them in the following week.

18. She **disdained** him because he was an unrepentant chauvinist.

19. Rolls Royce and Jaguar are established British marques, epitomizing automotive **panache**.

20. For centuries philosophers have **cogitated** upon the reason for our existence.

21. If the school doesn't receive additional funding soon, many of its most important programs will be in **jeopardy**.

22. Detectives need to be tough and **exacting** to avoid missing clues.

SYNONYM SENTENCES

1. Following a short walk, she said that she was having heart palpitations and that she should see a **cardiologist**.

2. Before I reach a decision, I will need to **cogitate** and consider the relevant data carefully.

3. We stood for the **duration** of their wedding ceremony, and when it was over I couldn't wait to find a couch to crash on.

4. Thunder scares Dakota, so I tried my best to **quell** his fear of the storm.

5. Looking at a paw print on the forest path, the ranger said, "From the size of this impression, we can **surmise** that this mountain lion was about six feet in length."

6. It is **ironic** that when she studies exceptionally hard for an exam, she'll usually earn a lower grade than when she studies less intensely.

7. These late nights studying are **exacting** a toll on me.

8. He and his father shared a **poignant** moment when they embraced one another for the first time in ten years.

9. Her father told her to stop hanging around with the teachers and to spend time with her **peers**.

10. While today's movie heroes use brute force to win the day, the leading men of classic movies always succeeded via their wits and **panache**.

11. He didn't want to **jeopardize** his chances of getting a car for graduation, so he made sure that he was always home by curfew.

12. While putting some new furniture together, I couldn't get one of the nuts to screw onto its bolt, so I put oil on it to reduce the **friction**.

13. Her blister was beginning to **fester**, so I told her to go see the nurse.

14. He was **forlorn** over the loss of his puppy and we couldn't cheer him up.

15. However, he was **elated** when he got home and his mom told him that she had found the puppy hiding in one of the closets.

16. Our coach **extolled** the benefits of a healthy diet and regular exercise.

17. She also implored us to **refrain** from smoking.

18. He said that although the project was a **colossal** failure, he would get back on his feet and try again.

19. Her relationship with her mom is **tempestuous** because they are so much alike.

20. My dad asked my friends to **refrain** from eating all of the chocolate in the house every time they came over.

21. He treats them with **disdain** whenever they drop by.

22. I think he's mentally **debilitated**; it's only chocolate.

THE ARTICLE

1. (b) After considering the other tracks on *Vocab Rock*, the author has deduced that "The Letter" is the most touching of all of the songs.

2. (d) Avon's graduate is dejected because his love went off to study medicine.

3. (b) It is paradoxical that the euphoria of love can be impaired by conflict.

4. (a) The couple's love at risk, the graduate ponders his options.

5. (c) The graduate wonders whether or not he can endure the frustration of being separated from his girlfriend.

6. (a) Avon's protagonist reflects on the enormity of deciding whether or not to end their relationship.

7. (d) The graduate is passionate about his love and praises her flair and sense of style.

8. (c) Avon's character repeats a phrase that his contemporaries would understand.

9. (b) The graduate increasingly misses his girlfriend and he cannot subdue his longing for her.

10. (d) Although it is a difficult decision, the graduate concludes that he and his girlfriend should break up.

UPSIDE DOWN

SYNONYM MATCHING

(f)	Calamity	disaster	(c)	Incur	sustain
(o)	Celerity	speed	(q)	Inverted	upturned
(k)	Chaos	disorder	(d)	Jostle	bump
(r)	Constellations	assemblage	(m)	Jubilation	celebration
(i)	Defied	disregard	(z)	Occur	transpire
(a)	Deviant	abnormal	(h)	Panorama	view
(n)	Disconcerting	disturbing	(w)	Peripheral	outer
(v)	Equanimity	composure	(e)	Reside	live
(b)	Gaze	stare	(l)	Resplendent	dazzling
(s)	Glimmer	gleam	(j)	Saturnine	gloomy
(y)	Impact	influence	(p)	Thaumaturgy	magic
(x)	Incontrovertibly	unquestionably	(u)	Trepidation	anxiety
(g)	Incredulous	skeptical	(t)	Unscathed	unharmed

sentence completion

1. He **defied** the odds and went on to become a champion.

2. At the concert we **jostled** our way through the crowd for a position at the foot of the stage.

3. Miraculously, the dog was **unscathed** after being hit by the bike.

4. She often paid her bills after their due date and **incurred** many late fees as a result.

5. **Chaos** broke out as the agitated crowd was jostled by the stadium ushers.

6. The company was struck by a series of **calamities**—executive fraud, a massive recall, and a class-action suit—all of which led to its bankruptcy.

7. Sitting on a dune above the beach, he **gazed** out at the ocean and admired the panorama.

8. She's very calm in difficult situations; you have to respect her **equanimity**.

9. The crowd was **jubilant** as each massive balloon rose out of the staging area and joined the Thanksgiving Day parade.

10. During the nineteenth century it was popular to visit circular exhibit halls that displayed **panoramic** paintings of renowned places or events.

11. Crossing the Golden Gate Bridge on a clear night, you can see the city lights **glimmering** in the distance.

12. Sparkling like a pile of diamonds a hundred miles away, Los Angeles is a **resplendent** beacon.

13. Despite the proof, he was **incredulous** and refused to believe that he was raised by wolves.

14. The **celerity** of the earth's rotation is 1,070 miles per hour.

15. Humanity's inability to behave humanely is very **disconcerting**.

16. The **constellation** the Big Dipper is a group of stars that look like a giant pot in the sky.

17. Their prior partnership was very frustrating, so he approached his new collaboration with the artist with some **trepidation**.

18. **Deviant** behavior is not socially acceptable.

19. Her grandparents now **reside** in Florida.

20. They were looking for **incontrovertible** proof of his complicity.

21. A wizard is skilled in **thaumaturgy**.

22. It was awesome; the rollercoaster track turned upside down and **inverted** the cars as we flew into a sharp turn.

23. A stolid woman, she always wore a **saturnine** expression on her face.

24. Watching a horror movie in a theater, I was scared senseless when I caught something move quickly through my **peripheral** vision.

25. It doesn't matter how many times I reboot my computer, glitches keep **occurring**.

26. Meteorites hit the moon regularly, leaving its surface pockmarked with **impact** craters.

SYNONYM SENTENCES

1. Her husband better drive with **celerity** or she'll have the baby in their car.

2. His **saturnine** gaze lays bare his life's hardships.

3. Not knowing what to expect, she approached the exam with **trepidation**.

4. When World War II ended, **jubilant** crowds packed Times Square.

5. For those who reach Mount Everest's summit, it must be sublime to take in the **panorama** of the entire world below you.

6. Remarkably, he was **unscathed** after falling down the stairs.

7. The facts prove her statements to be **incontrovertible**.

8. Flying over the shore on a bright summer day, I looked down and saw the beachgoers' sunglasses **glimmer** like mirrors scattered across the sand.

9. Although the Web doesn't appear to have a physical form, it is actually a vast **constellation** of interconnected computers.

10. The protesters **defied** the government and staged a sit-in near the capital.

11. The subway riders **jostled** one another as they made their way out of the crowded station.

12. Medieval tales often describe astonishing, **thaumaturgical** events.

13. I hate when I bring my car in to be repaired for an intermittent problem and when I get to the shop, it doesn't **occur**.

14. He decided to **reside** in the city because it was close to his job.

15. Her classic 'Vette was **resplendent** in bright white livery with blue racing stripes.

16. Her mom said, "Stop **gazing** out the window and finish your homework!"

17. We had so much work to do for the fete that we only took care of the essentials; we blew off doing anything that was **peripheral**.

18. His house was in a state of complete **chaos** after that party.

19. It wouldn't have been such a **calamity** if his parents hadn't come back from their vacation early.

20. It was pretty **disconcerting** to be standing there while they chewed him out.

21. They were **incredulous** that he ignored their instructions not to have anyone over.

22. I think what they were most upset about was the **inverted** ice cream truck in the garage.

23. This episode is definitely going to have a huge **impact** on his social life for a few months.

24. His dad, who's pretty melodramatic, yelled, "You have **incurred** my wrath!"

25. I can't believe that he handled it all with such **equanimity**.

26. We don't understand what they're so mad about; it's not like he's **deviant** or anything like that.

THE ARTICLE

1. (c) A catastrophe was going to befall Mia.

2. (d) The author is very happy that Mia did not pass on.

3. (a) On a beautiful summer evening Mia caught a glimpse of a car that was going to hit her.

4. (b) She was in a state of disbelief that some joker just ran a stop sign and was about to plow into her.

5. (c) She was fearful of the impending collision.

6. (d) Despite her fear of the coming collision, she remained level-headed and thought quickly.

7. (b) The oncoming car smashed into her car, throwing it sideways at great speed.

8. (a) Her car slid sideways with celerity, smashed into a hydrant, and overturned.

9. (c) When Mia opened her eyes, she was overturned, suspended by her seatbelt.

10. (d) Beating the odds, Mia was miraculously unhurt, incurring only a few bruises.

11. (a) Following the accident, Mia was happy.

12. (b) She shoved her way out of her seatbelt and fell onto the ceiling.

13. (a) Delirious but unscathed, Mia admired the stars shimmering in the night sky.

MOVE IT

SYNONYM MATCHING

(h)	Beset	inundated	(q)	Frolic	play	
(i)	Cavort	horse around	(b)	Gambol	bound	
(e)	Clout	influence	(f)	Grasp	understand	
(o)	Context	circumstances	(l)	Impression	perception	
(p)	Devotion	commitment	(a)	Indiscretion	tactlessness	
(j)	Distraction	disturbance	(g)	Induce	pressure	
(d)	Eternity	infinity	(s)	Resolve	solve	
(c)	Euphoric	elated	(t)	Rig	manipulate	
(k)	Fete	party	(n)	Sublime	transcendent	
(r)	Fret	worry	(m)	Symbiotic	mutually beneficial	

sentencecompletion

1. She was **euphoric** after finishing the SATs.

2. He couldn't **grasp** the ideas presented in the article.

3. The neighbor's party was **distracting** me from my homework.

4. She told him that he needed to **resolve** the problem today.

5. The **fete** to celebrate graduation is being held at my house.

6. He tried to make a good **impression** on his girlfriend's parents.

7. In the 1950s Congress investigated game shows that were suspected of being **rigged**.

8. Taken out of **context**, the senator's sound bite made him appear ridiculous.

9. **Cavorting** at the fete, the guys tossed their girlfriends in the pool.

10. His bragging went on and on; it lasted for an **eternity**.

11. Puppies like to **frolic** in the open grass.

12. The protesters **induced** her to stop wearing fur by telling her about all of the cute little animals that she would save.

13. Edgar Allen Poe, one of English literature's most renowned authors and a tragic figure, was **beset** by turmoil during his life and died penniless and alone.

14. Following the revelations of his affair with an intern, former President Clinton became known for his **indiscretions**.

15. The dancers **gamboled** across the stage.

16. The queen is regarded as a political figure, although she has no real political **clout**.

17. A healthy marriage is a **symbiotic** relationship.

18. Man, the beats we heard at the show took you to another place and time; they were **sublime**.

19. I told him, "Don't sit there **fretting** about Thursday's exam. Go study!"

20. Martin Luther King **devoted** his life to achieving racial equality.

SYNONYM SENTENCES

1. The children are **frolicking** in the yard.

2. The street performers **gamboled** across the plaza.

3. He created a **distraction** while she slipped out the back door.

4. My boss says that it doesn't hurt to have friends with **clout**.

5. We watched a beautiful sunset the other evening; it was **sublime**.

6. The kids were **cavorting** in the backyard.

7. He expressed his **devotion** to his girlfriend by proposing.

8. Parents often **fret** about their children.

9. Although the commercials were only 2 minutes long, it felt as though they went on for an **eternity**.

10. Calculus isn't really that hard to **grasp**.

11. After looking at the instructions, I have a pretty good **impression** of what I need to do.

12. The two sisters were forced to **resolve** their differences.

13. He was **euphoric** after receiving his acceptance letter to law school.

14. Urban communities worldwide are **beset** by air pollution.

15. She helped him with his homework, and he helped her with her move; their relationship was **symbiotic**.

16. If you understand the **context** in which the article was written, its point is clear.

17. They **induced** him to do the stunt by offering him a pile of cash.

18. It is against the law to **rig** the lottery.

19. Dumb criminals tend to be **indiscrete**, which makes them easy to catch.

20. The **fete** is at the club on 11th Street and 4th Avenue.

THE ARTICLE

1. (b) The guys have a mutually beneficial relationship.

2. (d) It is obvious that they are dedicated to entertaining people.

3. (c) Troy expressed that it took a lot of effort to write the song.

4. (a) Ed found it hard to find words that fit the circumstances of the song.

5. (d) They didn't let anything inhibit the progress of their work.

6. (d) They want to get listeners to dance and party.

7. (b) The guys said that "Move It" is a party track and it fosters an upbeat mood.

8. (c) The theme of "Move It" is easily understood.

9. (a) Ed and Troy want to get into the music industry.

10. (b) Ed and Troy trust that they won't be as careless as other successful artists.

11. (b) Troy and Ed want more chances to record.

12. (d) The guys want to make great music.

13. (d) They want their tracks to be enjoyed by audiences forever.

Acquiesce Amorous Aroma Awkward Consummate
Conversely Deleterious Delirium Ecstasy Enamored Futile
Incantation Inevitably Infatuation Inimitable Interminable
Intuit Laborious Prosimity Reticence Senescent Shroud
Situation Synchronously Tortuous Tranquility Acquiesce
Amorous Aroma Awkward Consummate Conversely
Deleterious Delirium Ecstasy Enamored Futile Incantation
Inevitably Infatuation Inimitable Interminable Intuit Laborious
Prosimity Reticence Senescent Shroud Situation
Synchronously Tortuous Tranquility Acquiesce Amorous
Aroma Awkward Consummate Conversely Deleterious
Delirium Ecstasy Enamored Futile Incantation Inevitably
Infatuation Inimitable Interminable Intuit Laborious Prosimity
Reticence Senescent Shroud Situation Synchronously
Tortuous Tranquility Acquiesce Amorous Aroma Awkward
Consummate Conversely Deleterious Delirium Ecstasy
Enamored Futile Incantation Inevitably Infatuation Inimitable
Interminable Intuit Laborious Prosimity Reticence Senescent
Shroud Situation Synchronously Tortuous Tranquility
Acquiesce Amorous Aroma Awkward Consummate
Conversely Deleterious Delirium Ecstasy Enamored Futile
Incantation Inevitably Infatuation Inimitable Interminable
Intuit Laborious Prosimity Reticence Senescent Shroud
Situation Synchronously Tortuous Tranquility Acquiesce
Amorous Aroma Awkward Consummate Conversely
Deleterious Delirium Ecstasy Enamored Futile Incantation
Inevitably Infatuation Inimitable Interminable Intuit Laborious
Prosimity Reticence Senescent Shroud Situation
Synchronously Tortuous Tranquility Acquiesce Amorous
Aroma Awkward Consummate Conversely Deleterious
Delirium Ecstasy Enamored Futile Incantation Inevitably
Infatuation Inimitable Interminable Intuit Laborious Prosimity
Reticence Senescent Shroud Situation Synchronously
Tortuous Tranquility Acquiesce Amorous Aroma Awkward
Consummate Conversely Deleterious Delirium Ecstasy
Enamored Futile Incantation Inevitably Infatuation Inimitable

Rodney Willie

EPHEMERAL DAYS

SYNONYM MATCHING

(e)	Abscond	escape	(a5)	Flagrant	blatant
(o)	Ambled	strolled	(a)	Haze	mist
(i)	Antiquity	ancient time	(g)	Impart	tell
(t)	Appraise	evaluate	(q)	Intrigued	curious
(x)	Beatific	virtuous	(a3)	Licentious	immoral
(k)	Cacophony	noise	(p)	Linger	loiter
(a4)	Captivating	entrancing	(d)	Modesty	reserve
(y)	Conception	notion	(b)	Novelty	newness
(a6)	Confounded	perplexed	(m)	Odyssey	journey
(z)	Dissuade	discourage	(a2)	Perceive	notice
(s)	Elated	overjoyed	(w)	Profusion	overabundance
(h)	Embark	begin	(a1)	Prolong	extend
(u)	Endure	persist	(f)	Sojourn	visit
(l)	Enigmatic	mysterious	(v)	Solemnly	seriously
(j)	Ephemeral	fleeting	(r)	Survey	review
(n)	Erroneously	wrongly	(c)	Vague	unclear

sentencecompletion

1. He had the painting **appraised** and was surprised to learn that it was very valuable.

2. It is easy to see (and hear) how the **cacophony** of sounds in a big city can overwhelm some people.

3. Pablo Picasso, a painter who often portrayed people's eyes on the same side of their heads, is known for his **enigmatic** style.

4. Her **beatific** smile is angelic.

5. The **haze** made it difficult for the driver to see what was ahead.

6. They **embarked** for the Bahamas via JFK International Airport.

7. We decided to **prolong** our date by going dancing after we saw the movie.

8. She **erroneously** believed that she would pass English, but she'll be retaking the class during summer school.

9. The professor **imparted** some of his accumulated wisdom to the class.

10. Although my friend felt he would wind up flipping burgers, the principal was determined to **dissuade** him from dropping out.

11. After the doctors told her that she had six months to live, she **confounded** them by overcoming her illness.

12. I **ambled** down the beach, stopping occasionally to pick up seashells.

13. Sometimes, it's the **ephemeral** nature of summer relationships that makes them work.

14. I saw an animated cat-and-mouse flick that **flagrantly** ripped off some classic cartoons.

15. The painting was so beautiful that I couldn't take my eyes off of it; it was **captivating**.

16. Skulking through the alleyway, the jewel thieves **absconded** with the gems they stole.

17. It is extraordinary that William Shakespeare's works continue to **endure** century after century.

18. She was very demure, and her **modesty** prevented her from talking about her achievements.

19. He had never encountered such a device before and was **intrigued** by its novelty.

20. She got lost on her way here because the directions were too **vague**.

21. Recognizing that it was futile to try following the vague directions, she said, "Well, I have no **conception** of how to get there."

22. After my friend opened a ketchup bottle by using his belly button, I said, "Well, that was certainly a **novel** approach."

23. The readers **solemnly** recited the names of those who lost their lives in the fire.

24. Before we rented a tent for the party, I went out to **survey** the backyard to determine out how it would best fit.

25. It was one of those great ephemeral love affairs—two people meeting one another during a brief **sojourn**, enjoying each other's company, and then continuing on their separate paths.

26. Las Vegas, which is known as "Sin City," is playing up its **licentious** image to attract tourists.

27. Opening the stereo cabinet, I found a **profusion** of wires and realized that I had no idea what I was doing.

28. The Pyramids in Giza, Egypt, date to **antiquity**.

29. Trying to get her laptop fixed, she spoke with four customer service reps, three different technicians, and a software engineer; it was an **odyssey**.

30. I may be wrong, but they look like they're up to no good, just **lingering** in the hallway, furtively looking back and forth.

31. If they're supposed to be in the building, I **perceive** that they may be waiting for someone to come with the keys to the apartment.

32. She was **elated** when she found out that she had won the car.

SYNONYM SENTENCES

1. He wanted to **appraise** the situation before deciding what to do.

2. Despite her great wealth she was a very **modest**, understated person.

3. I haven't lived in Paris for years, but the memories of my time there **endure**.

4. Getting this company started has been an **odyssey**.

5. At the earliest opportunity, the wife and I are going for a quick **sojourn** to South Beach.

6. She wanted to tan, but a light **haze** was blocking the sun.

7. When he knocked over all of the pots that had been drying, his mom, jarred by the sound of crashing cookware, yelled, "What is that **cacophony**?"

8. Despite his efforts to get her to leave for someplace safe, he couldn't **dissuade** her from staying.

9. We looked at the photo she took of what she told us was the Loch Ness Monster, but all we could make out was the **vague** outline of something in the water.

10. Slipping into the night, the spies **absconded** with a copy of the secret launch codes.

11. The burlesque dancers **licentiously** draped themselves over the show's host.

12. In a low, **solemn** voice, the doctor informed her that her condition was inoperable.

13. With roots that reach back thousands of years, the world's major religions all date to **antiquity**.

14. I was too excited to sleep because today we're **embarking** on our journey.

15. He's been working on the project for years but it was originally her **concept**.

16. After their argument, she **erroneously** believed that he would wait for her.

17. I love to **amble** through interesting parts of the city that I don't know yet.

18. Given that his car was gone, I **perceived** that he had already left.

19. I was intrigued by the **novelty** of the technology.

20. The recording star **confounded** her critics by becoming more popular than ever.

21. He was **elated** when he received his acceptance letter from MIT.

22. After the tornado she came out of the cellar to **survey** the damage to the house.

23. On our trek through the Amazon, a native priest **imparted** his wisdom to us.

24. Poetry has always been **enigmatic** to her, and she can never figure out what the author is trying to say.

25. The new technology was **intriguing** and sparked my curiosity.

26. Lazy summer days are always too **ephemeral**.

27. I did everything I could to **prolong** my afternoon nap on Sunday, but the din outside kept waking me up.

28. There is a **profusion** of diet gimmicks on the market, but that doesn't mean that any of them work.

29. Dakota is the cutest little kid with the most **beatific** smile.

30. I urged her to stay inside where it was safe, but she **flagrantly** ignored my advice and walked out into the hurricane.

31. I always like to **linger** after a movie ends to see if the director did anything interesting during the credits, like include intriguing outtakes.

32. She was **captivated** by the film's lush imagery.

The ARTICLE

1. (d) The authors were hanging around the production studio.
2. (c) She thought of the title prior to writing the song.
3. (a) Nina likes a word that means "short-lived."
4. (b) Nina was on vacation when she began writing the lyrics.
5. (a) Ideas and words for the song were written at different times.
6. (a) She found the city magnificent and rich in history.
7. (c) She was excited to begin her visit.
8. (b) Nina had a modest knowledge of the city's outstanding architecture.
9. (b) She was struck by the multiplicity of cultures and the restraint of its citizens.
10. (c) Compared to New York, she found Barcelona somewhat difficult to understand.
11. (d) Nina was captivated by Barcelona and savored walking its bustling streets.
12. (a) Nina would have liked to stay in Barcelona, but she needed to get home.
13. (b) Nina was sad to leave Barcelona, but she was compelled to do so.
14. (d) She expects that she will remember Barcelona for an indefinite period.

Acquiesce Amorous Aroma Awkward Consummate
Conversely Deleterious Delirium Ecstasy Enamored Futile
Incantation Inevitably Infatuation Inimitable Interminable
Intuit Laborious Prosimity Reticence Senescent Shroud
Situation Synchronously Tortuous Tranquility Acquiesce
Amorous Aroma Awkward Consummate Conversely
Deleterious Delirium Ecstasy Enamored Futile Incantation
Inevitably Infatuation Inimitable Intuit Laborious
Prosimity Shroud Situation
Synch. uiesce Amorous
Aroma ely Deleterious
Delirium ation Inevitably
Infatuatio rious Prosimity
Reticence Synchronously
Tortuous T ma Awkward
Consumma um Ecstasy
Enamored F n Inimitable
Interminable Senescent
Shroud Stu Tranquility
Acquiesce A sunmate
Conversely D ed Futile
Incantation In minable
Intuit Laborious ent Shroud
Situation Synchr Tranquility Acquiesce
Amorous Aroma Kward Consummate Conversely
Deleterious Delirium Ecstasy Enamored Futile Incantation
Inevitably Infatuation Inimitable Interminable Intuit Laborious
Prosimity Reticence Senescent Shroud Situation
Synchronously Tortuous Tranquility Acquiesce Amorous
Aroma Awkward Consummate Conversely Deleterious
Delirium Ecstasy Enamored Futile Incantation Inevitably
Infatuation Inimitable Interminable Intuit Laborious Prosimity
Reticence Senescent Shroud Situation Synchronously
Tortuous Tranquility Acquiesce Amorous Aroma Awkward
Consummate Conversely Deleterious Delirium Ecstasy
Enamored Futile Incantation Inevitably Infatuation Inimitable

Nina Zeitlin

SUBLIME

SYNONYM MATCHING

(j)	Apathetic	indifferent	(c)	Muddled	jumbled
(d)	Barren	desolate	(w)	Palpitating	throbbing
(l)	Basking	sunbathing	(u)	Quiver	shake
(h)	Berate	scold	(t)	Random	haphazard
(v)	Deluded	deceived	(s)	Savor	relish
(q)	Din	noise	(m)	Scurry	scamper
(b)	Finesse	skill	(a)	Shimmer	twinkle
(r)	Gait	pace	(p)	State	condition
(g)	Hoax	trick	(n)	Sublime	perfect
(o)	Iridescent	glow	(f)	Succumb	yield
(e)	Languid	relaxed	(i)	Unravel	disentangle
(k)	Lucid	coherent	(x)	Vindicate	exonerate

sentence completion

1. Looking down at the street from my office window, I watched the people **scurry** as the rain began to fall.

2. She **berated** him for telling her that aliens stole his homework.

3. Questioning him, she thought that his story would **unravel**.

4. Positive that his tale was a **hoax**, she sent him to the principal.

5. Then, all of a sudden, an unusual light with an **iridescent** glow came through the window.

6. We couldn't believe our eyes, but a tall figure that **shimmered** in the light stepped in through the window and handed the teacher his homework.

7. **Vindicated** by the extraordinary events, he came back to the classroom and said, "I told you that aliens stole my homework!"

8. After a great day of swimming and basking in the sun, we ambled down the beach at a **languid** pace to head back to our hotel.

9. My grandfather was sent to the hospital with heart **palpitations**.

10. The Confederate army **succumbed** to Union forces in March 1865.

11. When I go to the beach, all I want to do is **bask** in the sun.

12. Photographs of Mars depict a **barren**, rocky landscape.

13. As the bear slowly approached us, we began to **quiver** with fear.

14. Unable to finish a sentence, it was obvious that her thoughts were **muddled**.

15. After sampling a very fine vintage bottle of wine, the connoisseur remarked, "What a **sublime** finish!"

16. Never having encountered such an extraordinary vintage before, he **savored** every drop.

17. His mom said, "He is completely **deluded** if he expects me to pick up after him for the rest of his life."

18. We cannot become **apathetic** and take democracy for granted.

19. I couldn't keep up with my sister as we walked downtown because she has a much longer **gait** than I do.

20. He gave a clear and **lucid** argument supporting states' rights.

21. The speaker was forced to yell over the **din** of the crowd.

22. After 9/11 it isn't uncommon to be subjected to a **random** search at an airport.

23. But, I'm sad to say, that is today's **state** of affairs.

24. He forgot her name, but handled the situation with such **finesse** that she

SYNONYM SENTENCES

1. She only slept for a few hours last night and woke up completely **muddled** this morning.

2. Her beautiful hair **shimmered** in the sunlight.

3. He found the hose in knots but **unraveled** it so he could water the plants.

4. It was an elaborate **hoax**, which took months to prepare.

5. Cold-blooded animals need to **bask** in the sun to maintain their body temperatures.

6. Acquitted by the jury, the defendant was thrilled to be **vindicated**.

7. During hot, humid summer days, I like to keep a **languid** pace.

8. He lacked **finesse**, but he always got the job done.

9. Sometimes, given the overwhelming crises here at home, it's hard not to be **apathetic** about problems elsewhere.

10. The horse trainer was irate when he found out that the mare he just bought was **barren**.

11. As the Grammy results were read, she **quivered** with anticipation.

12. Following her fall down the stairs, he asked her how many fingers he was holding up to see if she was **lucid**.

13. The mouse **scurried** across the kitchen floor.

14. The **din** of the traffic kept me awake all night.

15. There is something **sublime** about every morning's sunrise.

16. I'm always in awe of the sun's **iridescence** as it breaches the horizon.

17. The horse trotted at a moderate **gait**.

18. To me, events seem pretty **random**, and—good or bad—you never know what's going to happen next.

19. After he found out that he she conned him, he said, "I can't believe that I was so **deluded**!"

20. My heart was **palpitating** after the 4-mile run.

21. The teacher **berated** her for coming late to class.

22. When he awoke in a strange and unfamiliar place, he was in a very confused **state**.

23. Exhausted from battling the disease for years, my grandmother **succumbed** and passed away this morning.

24. Great achievements are always comprised of small feats, so I **savor** every accomplishment, no matter how insignificant it might seem.

THE ARTICLE

1. (b) The author was running to get out of the rain and couldn't catch his breath.

2. (a) The doorway light cast a glow that twinkled in the rain drops on the author's jacket.

3. (d) He savors the odd tranquility that occurs when it rains heavily in New York.

4. (c) He was kidding himself when he thought that the rain would stop soon.

5. (b) Keith gave in to the fact that the rain was not going to let up.

6. (a) The author was coherent but largely unmotivated.

7. (c) The author was having one of those days when you can't get it together.

8. (d) The author was hoping the day would improve, but he didn't expect it to.

9. (b) No matter how down you get, if you keep it together, you can come through.

10. (a) Once Keith got to the studio, he felt better.

11. (c) The author appreciates being part of something creative.

12. (d) He had energy and trembled when he heard a high note over other music in the studio.

13. (b) The author chastised himself for letting the rain undermine his mood.

14. (a) The kitchen cabinet did not contain any coffee.

WIDE OPEN SPACES

SYNONYM MATCHING

(a3)	Abstain	refrain	(j)	Manifest	apparent
(i)	Affliction	cause of suffering	(d)	Nemesis	archenemy
(h)	Conjuration	witchcraft	(g)	Nostalgic	wistful
(r)	Contagion	source of infection	(n)	Obnoxious	insufferable
(a5)	Credence	credibility	(a6)	Obscure	vague
(l)	Demure	reserved	(a2)	Obtuse	stupid
(a1)	Effervescent	fizzy	(a4)	Ominous	foreboding
(z)	Enamored	smitten	(o)	Pernicious	evil
(b)	Fallacy	falsehood	(m)	Plague	outbreak
(q)	Filament	thread	(a)	Plausible	credible
(x)	Fissure	crevice	(s)	Predilection	partiality
(f)	Flag	wane	(v)	Reconcile	settle
(e)	Flounder	falter	(p)	Refrain	avoid doing
(t)	Forgo	relinquish	(w)	Superfluous	extraneous
(k)	Grave	serious	(y)	Valor	bravery
(c)	Lucidity	clarity	(u)	Volatile	erratic

sentence completion

1. The general bestowed a medal on the private for his **valor** in battle.

2. The bird flu virus is a **contagion** that was thought only to affect chickens and other fowl but now appears to also be harmful to humans.

3. The Department of Homeland Security issued an **ominous** warning to be on the lookout for suspicious activity.

4. She decided to **forgo** her bonus and instead gave it to charity.

5. He was in **grave** condition after the accident.

6. She was always loud, crass, and **obnoxious**.

7. He plays the tenor sax and has a **predilection** for John Coltrane and jazz from the 1950s.

8. It goes without saying that every superhero needs a **nemesis** to battle.

9. "I'd like to believe that your grandmother ate your homework, but couldn't you at least try to give me a **plausible** explanation?"

10. Surprisingly, human beings' small toes are **superfluous** and do not help us to stand.

11. Some people are just **obtuse**—you can explain something to them a thousand times, but they still don't get it.

12. Although we couldn't stand one another, we sat down face to face and worked to **reconcile** our differences.

13. Around the holidays I become **nostalgic** for the Thanksgiving dinners that we use to have at my grandmother's house.

14. The hurricane first **manifested** as a tropical storm in the south Caribbean.

15. He was practiced in the art of **conjuration** and referred to himself as a *warlock*.

16. Mount St. Helens is a **volatile**, active volcano located 50 miles northeast of Portland, Oregon.

17. After she dumped him for being obnoxious, he made up **fallacious**, hurtful claims about her.

18. While perusing an **obscure** journal that was written around 1850, a researcher uncovered new information about Lincoln's hat.

19. Pressure in the volcanic vent decreased after steam was released through a new **fissure** in the bedrock.

20. Unable to agree on the details of any issue, the peace talks' negotiators are **floundering** in their effort to reconcile their positions.

21. Research shows that children are drinking coffee, but they should **abstain** from consuming large quantities of caffeine until after the age of 18.

22. In light of the fact that his grandmother likes to eat paper, there might be some **credence** to his claim that she ate his homework.

23. Compelled by an anxious electorate and no employment growth, the candidates have focused on the **flagging** job market.

24. The United Nations has asked China to **refrain** from imprisoning human rights activists.

25. Would-be terrorists are **plaguing** airlines with bomb hoaxes and other disruptions to their operations.

26. According to the Center for Disease Control, noise-induced hearing loss is currently the most common occupational **affliction**.

27. She recently became **enamored** with photography and now she never leaves the house without her camera.

28. Unfortunately, seniors often begin to lose their **lucidity** as they become older and the aging process accelerates.

29. Automotive lighting technology has made significant advances over the past few years, discarding incandescent **filaments** in favor of electro-reactive gases like xenon.

30. When monks first accidentally created champagne in the 1680s, its **effervescence** was an undesirable trait that was regarded as a sign of poor wine making.

31. Their group was reprimanded for spreading **pernicious**, hurtful rumors about other students.

32. Preparing to address the delegates, the keynote speaker adopted a **demure**, restrained tone of voice and a formal posture.

SYNONYM SENTENCES

1. I wish that she would **abstain** from blowing her nose into her shirt because she's grossing me out.

2. There isn't a **filament** of truth to his claim that he's the queen's son.

3. He had a difficult time responding to his opponent's arguments and **floundered** throughout the debate.

4. Dr. Evil is Austin Power's **nemesis**

5. Given the fact that there are an infinite number of galaxies, it is entirely **plausible** that there is intelligent life somewhere in the universe.

6. The band's tour was canceled due to **flagging** ticket sales.

7. She's a pathological liar and I don't put an ounce of **credence** in anything she has to say.

8. Don't you hate when you can't get a song's **refrain** out of your head even though you haven't heard it in three days?

9. My parents love my current girlfriend, but I think that she's too **demure** for my liking.

10. Recording her expenses when they occur makes it is easier for her to **reconcile** her checkbook with her bank statement.

11. The **contagion** was traced to a research lab that was active during the cold war.

12. The event's **effervescent** host welcomed everyone personally.

13. The prevalence of brutality and bloodshed on TV has the **pernicious** effect of desensitizing people to violence.

14. Despite its complexities, she described the process with great **lucidity**, which gave us a better understanding of how it would progress.

15. It is interesting that even the brightest people will believe almost any **fallacy** if it is repeated frequently enough.

16. Predicated upon **conjuration**, Vodun (also known as *Voodoo*) is a religion that has been practiced in West Africa for more than 6,000 years.

17. Since we don't have the data yet, we'll **forgo** meeting until next week.

18. An alien variety of seaweed is posing a **grave** threat to the indigenous species of the Mediterranean's sea bed.

19. Recent leading financial indicators have been extremely **volatile**, underscoring the uncertain state of the economy.

20. I thought that I had made my point clearly, but it seems that he was too **obtuse** to grasp it.

21. Her fiancé is totally **obnoxious**; the first time he came over he headed straight for the fridge and then whined that we didn't have any cheese.

22. She's been **plagued** by self-doubt and just can't seem to shake it.

23. The **affliction** is weakening his immune system, making him more susceptible to infection.

24. Due to the city's budget woes, a new round of service cuts and tax increases are **manifesting**.

25. Unencumbered by **superfluous** posturing, her performance was raw and inspiring.

26. Away at college, he was swept up by a wave of **nostalgia** and decided to call some old friends.

27. Although the score was tied, they won the match due to an old, **obscure** technicality.

28. They're so **enamored** with one another that the entire world around them could crumble and they would barely notice.

29. With an equal number of classes in favor of and against the proposed changes, a **fissure** in the student body was exposed.

30. A fearless warrior, Joan of Arc was renowned for her faith and **valor**.

31. Given the growing deficit and declining tax income, the budget situation appears **ominous**.

32. Considering her **predilection** for yellow, I was surprised that she bought a blue car.

ARTICLE

1. (c) The author believes that he may have found a foreboding trend in Nina's songs.

2. (d) Nina seems disposed to writing reflective songs about her bad relationships.

3. (b) She writes songs about relationships with men who aren't good for her.

4. (a) The author cannot square his image of Nina with her heated lyrics.

5. (d) The subject matter of Nina's songs may be considered volatile because she is describing men who are erratic.

6. (b) Nina's vibrant and sometimes decorous; her personality belies the resentment captured by her lyrics.

7. (a) It is possible that she is smitten with guys who are wrong for her, but she can't keep herself from dating loutish, stupid idiots.

8. (c) The author poses that Nina's courage encourages her to date jerks.

9. (a) Nina's ex-boyfriends put on a good face at first, then, once they're dating, problems arise as they begin to reveal their true nature.

10. (c) Their attraction to one another wanes and their relationship begins to struggle.

11. (b) Keith suggests that his inferences may be a misguided belief and he doesn't put much weight in his theories.

12. (d) Keith regards his analysis of Nina's work as extraneous, but he also says that there may be some truth to his inferences.

13. (c) The author questions his sanity and says that he should stop overanalyzing things.

Rocco DeCicco of The Mia Johnson Band

Notes

Notes